I0901789

Advent Can Still Change the World

Advent Can Still Change the World
Bringing Christmas Past into Christmas Present

Advent Can Still Change the World
978-1-7910-4194-6
978-1-7910-4195-3 eBook

Advent Can Still Change the World DVD
978-1-7910-4198-4

Also by Josh Scott:

Bible Stories for Grown-Ups: Reading Scripture with New Eyes

Context: Putting Scripture in Its Place

Parables: Putting Jesus's Stories in Their Place

Cross-Examined: Reading the Bible in Times of Division

Cover description: Appearing on a deep blue background, a gold torn-paper banner carries the title, *Advent Can Still Change the World,* beneath a small angel blowing a trumpet and a bright star. Below, a large Nativity silhouette filled with biblical text contains Mary, Joseph, and the infant Jesus beneath a stylized Bethlehem skyline. The subtitle, *Bringing Christmas Past into Christmas Present,* is centered below the Nativity. At the bottom, the magi approach from one side while shepherds with sheep approach from the other, with the author's name, Josh Scott, centered beneath them.

Josh Scott

Advent Can Still Change the World

Bringing Christmas Past *into* Christmas Present

Abingdon Press | Nashville

Advent Can Still Change the World
Bringing Christmas Past into Christmas Present

Library of Congress Control Number: 2026942454
978-1-7910-4194-6

MANUFACTURED IN THE UNITED STATES OF AMERICA

For my parents,
Arthur G. "Chip" Scott
and Lisa Joy King Scott,
who always knew how to make
Christmas memorable and magical.

CONTENTS

INTRODUCTION

Christmas Past

My first vivid, unforgettable Christmas memory comes from 1984. Why that Christmas, you ask? It wasn't the tinsel or those iconic bubble lights that adorned our tree, though I recall them. What seared this specific yuletide in my memory was the gift I found waiting for me under our tree on Christmas Eve night.

I was obsessed with a new cartoon/toy line that had been released that year called The Transformers. For the uninitiated, let me explain the absolute coolness of these toys. They were practically two toys in one—cars, planes, motorcycles, you get the picture—that transformed with a few quick moves into alien robots locked in a cosmic battle for dominance. There was one toy from the line in particular that was difficult to find anywhere; in the days before online shopping, you had to have the good luck of being in the right place at the right time. That toy would be, you probably guessed it, the Optimus Prime semi-truck. I longed for that toy like a deer pants for streams of water, I tell you.

That's why that Christmas made an unforgettable impression on that younger version of me. When we returned to our small trailer that sat near my grandparents' home, nestled under the tree in all its transforming glory was the elusive Optimus Prime. Santa had come through in a major way, and I will never forget just how it felt to see that toy waiting for me under the Christmas tree.

It was a few years later that I learned that all my Christmas joy had not been the result of a jolly old elf who was skilled at breaking and entering, even into houses without chimney access, but that it was, instead, my parents who curated all those gifts over the years. When I say they understood how to create unforgettable Christmas magic, that is an understatement. Perhaps their thoughtfulness during the season is why I, as a dad of five kids, receive the most holiday thrills not in opening gifts with my name on the tag, but in watching our kids' eyes light up and dance with excitement on Christmas mornings. Of course, Christmas is about so much more than presents, and we make sure our kids know that. Make no mistake, however, for kids, those wish-lists-come-true play a big part in making the season bright. There is no doubt that the care and generosity my parents displayed when I was a child have shaped the way I engage my own kids and the lengths to which my wife and I will go to track down that special gift they are hoping to find under the tree on Christmas morning.

I have come to understand that Christmases past—the way my parents did things, the traditions we developed, and the memories we made—have had a direct impact on how I approach these same things with my kids today. Christmases past are always intruding on Christmases present and shaping Christmases future.

That is the theme of this study—the way Christmas past still shapes Christmases present and future. Here, I am not referring to our own personal Christmas experiences, but to that first Christmas, to the birth of Jesus, and how his advent has and is transforming our lives, the world, and the future. In the pages that follow, we will examine the birth stories in the New Testament and discover some familiar and sometimes surprising insights. Before we begin that journey through these stories, I want to situate the details of Jesus's birth within the tradition of Scripture. How do we know anything about Jesus's birth? What are the sources from which we have shaped our carols, traditions, and Christmas pageants?

DATING AND SOURCES FOR THE BIRTH OF JESUS

We don't know the specific dates of the events in Jesus's life, but we can identify probable or possible time windows. For example, we don't know exactly when Jesus was born (but it most likely wasn't on December 25). Because the Gospel of Matthew places Jesus's nativity during the reign of Herod the Great, who died in 4 BCE, Jesus's birth date is commonly estimated to be between 6 and 4 BCE. While information related to his birth is limited, the range of possible dates for his death is more historically solid. According to all four canonical Gospels, early tradition, and the work of the Jewish historian Josephus, Jesus was executed under the Roman governorship of Pontius Pilate, and we know Pilate was stationed in Judea between 26 and 36 CE. So, Jesus was likely crucified sometime during that ten-year span. We can't attribute specific dates to Jesus's life and death; our best guess is that the window was between 6 BCE at the earliest and 36 CE at the very latest, with many scholars using 30 CE as a probable year for the Crucifixion.

Our sources for Jesus's birth stories are primarily the Gospels of Matthew and Luke, and they present vastly different narratives, which is why it is better to refer to the Christmas stories (plural), rather than a Christmas story (singular). Even then, the stories of his birth emerge decades after the events of his life. The earliest written materials available to us are the authentic letters of Paul, dated to the 50s to early 60s—some thirty years after Jesus's execution. In those letters, Paul never narrates or even mentions the birth of Jesus specifically. However, in Galatians, which scholars believe is one of his earliest letters, dated as early as 50 CE, Paul writes

> *When the fullness of time had come, God sent his Son, born of a woman, born under the law.*
>
> *(Galatians 4:4)*

Here, Paul makes two claims: (1) Jesus was "born of a woman," which is how everyone is born, and (2) he was "born under the law," meaning he was Jewish. According to Paul, Jesus was human and Jewish—not a groundbreaking claim. But one other statement from Paul should be added to that portrait. In Romans, one of his last letters, Paul says that Jesus was descended from a particular figure of the Jewish past:

> *Paul, a servant of Christ Jesus, called to be an apostle, set apart for the gospel of God, which he promised beforehand through his prophets in the holy scriptures, the gospel concerning his Son, who was descended from David according to the flesh and was declared to be Son of God with power*

> *according to the spirit of holiness by resurrection from the dead, Jesus Christ our Lord. . . .*
>
> *(Romans 1:1-4)*

Paul's claim is that Jesus was a Jew descended from the line of the great Jewish king, David. The phrase "according to the flesh" is just a way of saying, "This is his ancestor." This is no small claim: To be the descendant of David, in the sense that Paul uses it here, is to be the rightful Davidic ruler, the one who should occupy the throne of Israel. In the mid-first century, under Roman occupation, such words were treasonous. Rome didn't mind a client king who would expand and support their rule. Rome did, however, have a serious issue with a claimant to the throne who envisioned a different order for the world.

These two passages are the only passing references we have from Paul about the birth of Jesus. His letters contain no mention of Jesus's mother or any of the events that we connect with the Christmas stories. The only relative of Jesus that Paul names is James, whom he refers to as "the Lord's brother" (Galatians 1:19). It is apparent from Paul's letters that Jesus and James experienced a tense relationship, to say the least.

The next New Testament literature we have chronologically is the Gospel of Mark, which scholars date sometime between 70 and 73 CE. This might seem surprising because Matthew precedes Mark in the canonical order of the New Testament, but most scholars believe that Matthew was written after Mark. In fact, it can be demonstrated that Matthew uses more than 90 percent of Mark's words in his own Gospel. Apparently, copyright infringement wasn't an issue in the ancient world.

In Mark's story, we do not begin with Jesus's birth or infancy. Instead, Mark begins his narrative with Jesus as an adult, going out into the wilderness to be baptized by John the Baptizer. The only references to Jesus's origins in Mark are in a couple of passages in the first half of the Gospel. First, Mark locates Jesus as coming from Nazareth, an insignificant rural town in the region of Galilee in northern Israel:

> *In those days Jesus came from Nazareth of Galilee and was baptized by John in the Jordan.*
>
> *(Mark 1:9)*

Further, two chapters later, we find that Jesus's family has grown concerned about his well-being and intends to take him back home, away from the crowds. Jesus, however, responds by redefining familial relationships in the kingdom of God. They are less about biology and more about collaboration with Jesus:

> *Then he went home, and the crowd came together again, so that they could not even eat. When his family heard it, they went out to restrain him, for people were saying, "He has gone out of his mind."*
>
> *(Mark 3:20–21)*

> *Then his mother and his brothers came, and standing outside they sent to him and called him. A crowd was sitting around him, and they said to him, "Your mother and your brothers are outside asking for you." And he replied, "Who are my mother and my brothers?" And looking at those who sat around him, he said, "Here are my mother and my brothers! Whoever does the will of God is my brother and sister and mother."*
>
> *(Mark 3:31–35)*

The absence of any mention of Jesus's birth story is noticeable, considering how the later tradition develops, particularly in the

Gospel of Luke. Luke reports that Mary is visited by an angel who shares a message about just how remarkable this child will be. Mark seems completely unaware of, or uninterested in, any such event.

In Mark 6, we find Jesus teaching in his hometown synagogue, and many of his listeners were appalled by his teaching. They wonder where Jesus—this hometown boy they watched grow up—got his message and authority:

> *"Is not this the carpenter, the son of Mary and brother of James and Joses and Judas and Simon, and are not his sisters here with us?" And they took offense at him.*
>
> *(Mark 6:3)*

Here in Mark, for the first time chronologically in any writing that would become part of the New Testament, we learn the name of Jesus's mother. Mark also names four of Jesus's brothers and briefly mentions his sisters. Interestingly, Jesus is known to his hometown crowd as "the carpenter" (likely more like a stone mason than a woodworker) and as the "son of Mary." Perhaps some questions or rumors were swirling around about Jesus's paternity? Nonetheless, this pittance of information is all we get from Mark regarding biographical data on Jesus.

All that was about to change. Around a decade after Mark wrote, along came Matthew. He absorbed, with some variation, almost all of Mark and added his own contributions from other sources. Matthew's writing is dated to the 80s CE, likely more than eighty years after Jesus's birth and around fifty years after the Crucifixion. In his Gospel narrative, Matthew puts Jesus's birth center stage. Matthew begins with a genealogy that situates Jesus within his tradition as a child of Abraham and a son of David. While a list of names might seem a little boring and skippable, this particular list is of great importance for Matthew's understanding of Jesus. We will examine that more deeply in chapter 1.

Following the genealogy, we are introduced to Joseph, the earthly father of Jesus, who learns that his fiancée Mary is going to have a baby, and he is not the father. His intention to divorce her was reversed when a messenger from God spoke to him in a dream. That dream changed his mind and brought him into a bigger project than he could have ever imagined. Interestingly, the birth of Jesus is not narrated in Matthew, but simply mentioned in passing. Matthew's story wraps up with an episode that we will explore in chapter 4, the visit of the magi, with the unfolding drama that leads Herod to engage in a murderous rampage and Jesus and his family's exodus to and return from Egypt. Matthew makes no mention of Mary and Joseph's journey from Nazareth to Bethlehem. We may presume that they resided in Bethlehem before eventually relocating to Nazareth to avoid the danger of King Herod's heir, Archelaus.

Matthew then repeats from Mark the story of Jesus's family coming to see him. But in his telling, his family doesn't come to restrain him as recorded in Mark, but "to speak to him," which softens the situation a bit (Matthew 12:46). Also, instead of Jesus being referred to as "the carpenter," he is called "the carpenter's son" (Matthew 13:55).

Matthew's narrative would remain the only account of Jesus's birth for as little as ten to as many as possibly forty years. Then along came the Gospel of Luke, which was written between the late 80s and the early second century. The writer of this Gospel, who drew on Mark and possibly Matthew, among other sources, introduced a new version of Jesus's birth to the growing Nativity tradition.

For most of us, when we think of "the Christmas story," especially if we've attended a few Christmas pageants, we usually think of Luke's version (with the magi from Matthew tacked on to the end). We may even feel a nostalgic tug when reading about the events narrated in chapter 2—the journey from Nazareth to Bethlehem (omitted in Matthew's story) and the lack of available guest lodging that culminated in the newly born infant Jesus being laid in a manger. Luke also introduces us to the tradition of the visit of the shepherds, the circumcision and naming of the eight-day-old Jesus, and his presentation in the temple after forty days. There, he was officially named, and his destiny was affirmed by two prophets, Simeon and Anna. Luke's story leaves us with Jesus as a twelve-year-old in the temple, astonishing his listeners with his wisdom. Luke follows Matthew's version of Jesus's response to his family coming to see him, but he omits any mention of Jesus being "the carpenter," "the carpenter's son," or the "son of Mary."

That is all the Synoptic Gospels say about the birth of Jesus. John, probably written close in time to Luke, does not mention Jesus's birth directly. Instead, he begins, like the Greek translation of Genesis 1:1, with "In the beginning." In John's Gospel, Jesus is the enfleshment of the Word of God, which spoke creation into existence. However, although the author doesn't provide us with a proper birth narrative, he does make a few references to Jesus's parentage. First, in John 6, the author refers to Joseph as Jesus's father during a controversy about Jesus's teaching. Similar to Matthew and Luke, the crowd responds to Jesus's claim to be the "bread that came down from heaven" (John 6:41b) by questioning his origins:

> *They were saying, "Is not this Jesus, the son of Joseph, whose father and mother we know?"*
>
> *(John 6:42a)*

How can Jesus be "bread from heaven," they ask, because they know his family. He's a local boy; how could he have "come down from" somewhere else? Literalism always trips us up, doesn't it? Notice the verse mentions Jesus's mother, but in John, she is never called Mary. She is known only as "the mother of Jesus," and she is mentioned only three times. This reference in John 6 is the second time. The other two times she appears are the bookends of Jesus's ministry. She is the catalyst for the water-to-wine sign that marks the beginning of Jesus's public ministry (John 2:1-11), and she is at the cross as Jesus dies (John 19:25-27). Present but not named, Mary functions almost symbolically in John, representing the relationship between the Jesus movement and its Jewish roots.

A final mention in John that might raise our eyebrows occurs in John 8 during a conflict between Jesus and the crowd about being Abraham's descendants. During this tense exchange, the crowd responds to Jesus with an interesting statement:

> *They answered him, "Abraham is our father." Jesus said to them, "If you are Abraham's children, you would do what Abraham did, but now you are trying to kill me, a man who has told you the truth that I heard from God. This is not what Abraham did. You are indeed doing what your father does."*

> *They said to him, "We are not illegitimate children; we have one Father, God himself."*
>
> *(John 8:39-41)*

Like the comments about Jesus as "son of Mary" (Mark 6:3), the statement, "We are not illegitimate children," carries a lot of weight in this exchange. It feels more like an accusation about Jesus than a declaration about themselves. For Jesus, it is faithful action, not biology, that determines one's descent.

Outside these references in the four Gospels and Galatians, the New Testament makes no further mention of Jesus's birth and early life.[1] There are some noncanonical texts that purport to narrate the events of Jesus's birth; the Protoevangelium of James is the most well-known. This mid- to late-second-century text narrates the miraculous conceptions of both Mary and Jesus.

Clearly, Matthew and Luke provide the most, albeit limited, details about Jesus's birth and early life. What these two brief synopses make clear is that we are dealing with two distinct narratives, not a single, unified Christmas story. At the same time, both narratives present the birth of Jesus as a significant, transformative moment, not just in the history of Israel but for the entire world. In the Christ Child, "the hopes and fears of all the years are met."[2] These tales of Christmas past are significant because they inform Christmas present and shape future Christmases. If that is the case, the most important question we can ask is "What did these stories mean to their first hearers?" The second most important question is "What do these stories mean for us today and for future generations?" Both questions will shape the contents of this book.

ADVENT CAN STILL CHANGE THE WORLD

The season of the Christian calendar in which we reflect on these stories is called Advent. The season reflects the name; *Adventus*, in Latin, means *coming* or *arrival*. From what we can tell, Advent likely began in the fifth or sixth centuries as a season in which Christians prepared to celebrate the birth of Jesus, an event of the past with an emphasis on looking to the future advent of Jesus's return.

Advent is about patient and active waiting for a better world, a world of justice and peace, to be born. It is about patience because we cannot rush the process or avoid the difficulty involved in making a better world. It is also active because we are invited—challenged and called—to do everything we can to help midwife God's dream into human reality.

For those of us in the Northern Hemisphere, Advent arrives during winter, when daylight is scarce, the ground is frozen, and our year is coming to an end. Yet, on the Christian calendar, Advent is the beginning of a new liturgical year. However that determination was made, I think it's absolute genius; it captures the meaning of Advent beautifully. In the cold darkness, the Light of the world enters human history. When creation is most in the grip of death, Life is born.

Let me make one request before we continue. My guess is that most of us are familiar, or perhaps very familiar, with the Christmas stories and the events they narrate. As difficult as it can be, I want to invite you to bracket your assumptions, to hit pause on everything you think you know about these stories. I am convinced that these stories have so much to teach us about this work to which we are called, and sometimes we can become so familiar with them that they become unfamiliar. Don't be surprised, as we ground ourselves in the context of these stories, if we find many similarities to our own. The point of learning from Christmas past is, after all, to bring the vision and challenge of these stories into our own time and place. Advent, if we listen with openness and imagination, offers a message and vision that can still change the world.

CHAPTER 1

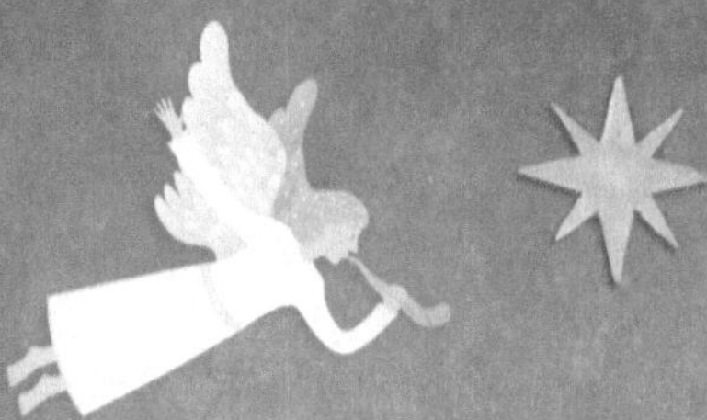

A NEW LOOK TO THE WHOLE WORLD

CHAPTER 1

A New Look to the Whole World

CHRISTMAS MEMORIES

My earliest memories of Christmas are inextricably tied to church experiences. The Octavia Freewill Baptist Church sat nestled in a holler in the hills of eastern Kentucky, just a mile or so from the little trailer in which I grew up. When I was a kid, that white, two-level cinder block building felt like an extension of my own home. I loved going to church, especially at Christmastime. Every year, kids would receive a "poke," a brown paper bag of fruit, nuts, and candy. I assumed everyone everywhere received the same. I only learned later that this was an Appalachian custom that began in the late 1800s, when such items were considered a treat, a bit more extravagant than your average grocery order.

We also put on our own Christmas pageant each year. Someone would assume the role of director, and other members of the church would be assigned roles, all of us playing our part to act out the story of Jesus's birth, the announcement to the shepherds, and the visit of the magi. I was so excited each year to discover what my role would be. One year, I turned in a particularly riveting performance as a sheep. People are still talking about it decades later.[1]

The original building burned during the Christmas season in 1984, and each year I hang on my own tree an ornament salvaged from the charred remains of what had been our community hub. Sometimes I swear I can still smell a hint of smoke on it. Placing that ornament in a prominent location each year reminds me of those dear people and that sacred place that shaped my earliest memories of both Jesus and Christmas.

My first interactions with the Christmas story came in a small Sunday school class in the basement of that church. It may surprise you to learn that we were a technologically sophisticated community in Appalachia in the 1980s: We didn't just read stories; we flannelgraphed them. If this is a new concept for you, just know that flannel boards were the height of creative technology in their time. Imagine a board of some kind, covered in flannel fabric, resting on an easel. The teacher would place cutouts of Bible characters, often made of flannel or sometimes paper backed with flannel or sandpaper, on the board and tell us a story while moving the figures around. It was telling and showing, and I was always glued to the action.

That is how the Christmas story was first brought to life for me, in a simple way that conveyed the birth of Jesus as a gift that would change the world. As the events of Jesus's birth unfolded before our eyes through two-dimensional cutouts, we learned the key details of the Christmas story: the annunciation to Mary, the journey to Bethlehem, the announcement to the shepherds, and the visit of the magi were all cemented into our imaginations. At an early age, I could offer, in detail, my understanding of how the Christmas story happened. Yet something was missing in that framework. We paid attention to the characters and their actions, but we didn't give any time or attention to the background against which they performed them. The facts of Jesus's life—when and where he was born or the political and economic realities of his world—were completely absent from our readings of these stories. That, I have come to learn, is unfortunate and significant because it causes us to miss a key piece of Jesus's story.

Jesus's birth did not happen in a vacuum. He was born in a particular time, in a particular place, in particular circumstances—all of which dramatically affected the events of his life. While I love and have a deep place of sentimental attachment to our Christmas hymns, the world into which he was born was not peaceful, still, or silent. The world that welcomed the first cries of the Christ Child was violent, chaotic, and tumultuous.

We are all shaped by our contexts. The times and places in which we live mold us in ways we don't always realize. Growing up in that Appalachian holler, my worldview was shaped by both the joy and the struggle of that context. No doubt, where and when you were born have played a similar developing role in your becoming. The same is true of Jesus. The world he entered was as much a character in his story—the first character, in fact—as Peter or Mary Magdalene. Just as the characters are placed on the felt board of the flannelgraph, so we, like Jesus, are placed onto our own background, not as quiet observers, but as active participants in shaping who we become and how our stories play out.

To fully appreciate the Christmas story now, we must first consider the story's background and context. To discover the meanings of Jesus's birth for our own time, we must first understand the challenge of his birth into a world that was not hospitable to his message. Specifically, when Jesus was born, Rome ruled his world, and Caesar ruled Rome. That is an indispensable fact for understanding his story. A central question, then, is this: What was the impact of Roman rule on Jesus's life? That will be the focus of this chapter.

BECOMING AUGUSTUS

One of the most glossed-over lines in Luke's Christmas story comes at the beginning of his narration of Jesus's birth. Before Joseph and Mary make the journey to Bethlehem, Luke situates the story of Jesus within the reign of Rome's first emperor, Caesar Augustus:

> *In those days a decree went out from Caesar Augustus that all the world should be registered. This was the first registration and was taken while Quirinius was governor of Syria. All went to their own towns to be registered.*
> *(Luke 2:1-3)*

Luke gets a little of his history wrong here, but I think we can cut him some slack. He was, after all, writing at least seventy and perhaps more than one hundred years after the birth of Jesus. The census he mentions did not happen at the time of Jesus's birth (often dated 4–6 BCE). This census was about counting people for the purpose of taxing them, which is never a popular idea, especially when your land and people are being controlled by a foreign empire that views people and property as a means to enrich itself. The other issue with Luke's use of this census is that a census wouldn't require people to travel to their ancestral homes to be counted. If you live and work around Nazareth, why would you be counted and taxed in Bethlehem? However, Luke is a creative writer, and he knows that the Messiah needs to be born in Bethlehem. He also knows that Jesus was from the small, insignificant town of Nazareth. The census becomes Luke's mechanism to bring Mary and Joseph to the right zip code for Jesus to be born.

The truth is, if Jesus of Nazareth had never been born, if the night sky had never exploded with a choir of angels announcing the good news of a savior's birth, history would still have recorded the story of a peace-bringing son of God who was credited with saving the world. His name was Octavian, who later became Caesar Augustus. While Luke's census history is a bit off, one detail that he gets spot on is that when Jesus was born, Caesar Augustus ruled his world. Augustus was not just any ruler; he was the first Roman emperor. He consolidated the republic's sprawling territories into an empire under his complete authority. Luke's mention of Augustus is a subtle reminder to his readers that Jesus entered a world defined by Rome's authority, bureaucracy, and control. A census forcing Mary and Joseph to make the journey from Nazareth to Bethlehem reflects this reality. It was a world where Augustus counted and cataloged human lives and in which decrees from a faraway ruler could move entire populations. By situating the Nativity within this context, Luke makes a profound statement: Jesus's birth was not only a religious event but also a historical one. It happened amid the real, often harsh, political realities of his world.

While almost everyone knows the name Jesus of Nazareth today, the marquee in his world had one name up in lights: Caesar Augustus. Who was he? How did the man born Gaius Octavius find himself in charge of most of the known world? And, most important, how does his story intersect with and impact the story of Jesus?

Before he was given the title Augustus, Octavian—the name modern historians use to refer to him before he became emperor—flew under the radar. He was often sick, physically weak, and didn't fit the mold of the impressive, battle-hardened leaders of the ancient world. His path to power was unlikely and hinged on the aftermath of an event that changed history: the assassination of his uncle, Julius Caesar.

On the Ides of March (March 15) 44 BCE, Julius Caesar was surprised and overwhelmed by a group of Roman senators who stabbed him some twenty-three times. The senators claimed they were engaging in an act of liberation, an attempt to save the Republic from a wannabe king. While Rome was a Republic, during times of emergency, the government would appoint a dictator, a temporary position giving one man supreme authority to deal with a crisis. Normally, Rome was run by two consuls who shared power, with the Senate acting as a check and balance; dictatorship was meant to be rare and, importantly, temporary. While Julius Caesar had held this role several times in the past, in February 44 BCE, a month before his assassination, the Senate made him "dictator for life." He didn't stage a military coup; instead, he used his influence, and perhaps some subtle arm-twisting, to secure his lifetime position via a legal act of the Senate. As dictator, Caesar could bypass most of the traditional Republican checks on his power. He could propose laws, appoint magistrates, control the treasury, and command armies without the usual limits that came with Republican offices. Many senators feared that this was the first step toward monarchy, making Caesar a king in all but title.

Then came March 15. The assassination of Julius Caesar threw Rome into utter chaos, and that chaos was soon followed by multiple civil wars that lasted thirteen years. Before his death, Caesar had, in his will, adopted his nephew Octavian to be his heir. When the dust settled, it was Octavian who stood alone as the leader of Rome. Shortly after, the Roman Senate conferred upon him the title Augustus, which means something like "the revered one." His victory in the civil wars that followed Caesar's assassination had not only saved Rome from collapse, but also, according to Roman poets, ushered in a new golden age for the Roman people. Augustus was no mere man; he was the embodiment of Roman ideals and values: order, victory, peace, stability, and tradition.

His ascension to the role of princeps (meaning "first person") blurred the lines between religion and politics. The Roman imperial cult honored the new Roman emperor as divine, especially in the eastern part of the empire, through public rituals, temples, and sacrifices, as a means of showing loyalty to the Roman state. To revere and, in some parts of the empire, worship Augustus was an act of patriotism.

This merging of politics and religion is clearly evident in an inscription discovered in the 1890s. The Priene Calendar Inscription is a Greek inscription dated to 9 BCE. It was rediscovered in the city of Priene, in what today is western Turkey. It records a decree from the Roman provincial assembly of Asia that announced that the birthday of Augustus would now mark the beginning of the new year. Augustus was not just in charge of the empire; now time itself would be ordered around him. For our purposes, it is the content of the inscription to which we need to pay attention.

> Since the providence that has divinely ordered our existence has applied her energy and zeal and has brought to life the most perfect good in Augustus, whom she filled with virtues for the benefit of mankind, bestowing him upon us and our descendants as a savior—he who put an end to war and will order peace, Caesar, who by his epiphany exceeded the hopes of those who prophesied good tidings, not only outdoing benefactors of the past, but also allowing no hope of greater benefactions in the future; and since the birthday of the god first brought to the world the good tidings residing in him. . . . For that reason, with good fortune and safety, the Greeks of Asia have decided that the New Year in all the cities should begin on 23rd September, the birthday of Augustus . . . and that the letter of the proconsul and the decree of Asia should be inscribed on a pillar of white marble, which is to be placed in the sacred precinct of Rome and Augustus.[2]

I imagine the language parallels to the story of Jesus are leaping off the page as we read each line. Caesar was sent by providence to be a savior and peace-bringer. His epiphany is good tidings (good news) for the whole world. He is also called divine, a god.

When the first followers of Jesus began to proclaim him as the risen Messiah, a savior and peace-bringer, and to share stories about his birth and the good news of great joy it brought, all of that had already been applied to Augustus. The Christmas stories and the story of Jesus as a whole are told in language and expressed through titles that expose the tension between two competing visions for the world: the Roman Empire and the kingdom of God.

WHAT'S IN A NAME?

Let's take a moment to explore some of the titles that were claimed by Augustus and held in subversive counterclaim by Jesus's followers. This list is not exhaustive, but it gives a brief survey of the key contested titles and how each group understood and applied them.

Son of God

After Julius Caesar's murder in March of 44 BCE, Rome was a political pressure cooker. In July of the same year, during funeral games held in Caesar's honor, a bright comet appeared in the daytime sky for about seven days. The Romans believed deeply in omens, and this one arrived at the perfect moment for the young Octavian. Because the comet was widely interpreted as Caesar's soul ascending to the heavens, Octavian used this fortuitous event as propaganda to bolster his claim to power and authority. It was proof that Caesar had taken his place among the gods, that he had become divine himself. Within two years, the rumor became true, as the Roman Senate declared Caesar, posthumously, as Divus Julius (the Divine Julius).

This move was central to Octavian's transformation into Augustus because now he was officially, legally, the son of a god (by adoption). He declared as much in the coinage he minted. Coins were how news spread in the ancient world. If you wanted to go viral, you wouldn't tweet about it; you'd make a coin. Many coins were minted featuring Augustus's face, and many featured celestial images such as comets and symbols related to Jupiter, the supreme god of the Roman pantheon. Augustus was not claiming to be Jupiter; he was claiming that he had Jupiter's divine favor and blessing. His rule was blessed and orchestrated by the gods, and Augustus himself was now, while living, considered divine. That was clear in the inscription, which declared Augustus to be the Divi Filius, or son of a god. Years later, during the reign of Augustus's successor, Tiberius, Jesus would be handed a similar coin bearing Tiberius's bust and a declaration of his divinity. This propaganda and these claims were not peripheral to Jesus's life. They were front and center.

Do you see, then, how the New Testament is in direct and dangerous tension with the Roman imperial propaganda? Twenty-three times in the Gospels and Paul's letters, Jesus, not Caesar, is identified as "God's son." For example, in the Gospel of Mark, when Jesus emerged from the waters of baptism and the heavens were torn in two, the voice of God declared that Jesus, not Caesar, was the beloved Son of God: "You are my Son, the Beloved; with you I am well pleased" (Mark 1:11). And when the man with unclean spirits encountered Jesus, he recognized Jesus and his authority as being connected to God: "When he saw Jesus from a distance, he ran and bowed down before him, and he shouted at the top of his voice, 'What have you to do with me, Jesus, Son of the Most High God?'" (Mark 5:6-7).

Shockingly, at the death of Jesus in Mark's Gospel, the declaration of Jesus as God's Son comes not from one of his followers or God but from a Roman centurion. One of Jesus's own executioners, seeing how Jesus died, comes to the realization that this is what it looks like and means to be the Son of God, giving oneself away for others: "Now when the centurion who stood facing him saw that in this way he breathed his last, he said, 'Truly this man was God's Son!'" (Mark 15:39).

Caesar's way is not it. Jesus, not Caesar, is the authentic Son of God, empowered and enlisted by God to embody the divine vision for the world. Caesar is an imposter, merely cosplaying as a son of god.

Lord

When the angels announced the birth of Jesus to the shepherds, they used particular, specific language to describe who this child was.

> *". . . to you is born this day in the city of David a Savior, who is the Messiah, the Lord."*
>
> *(Luke 2:11)*

That is just the tip of the iceberg for the title "Lord" being applied to Jesus. In the New Testament, Jesus is declared "Lord" almost three hundred times, with almost one hundred coming from Paul's letters. To be Lord, *kyrios* in Greek, meant one had authority to rule. Notice how Paul uses this title when he quotes what is likely an early hymn he has repurposed in his letter to the Philippians. The hymn begins by focusing on Jesus's obedience to being the kind of messiah God imagined, willing to be killed rather than to kill. Jesus and his message were rejected by Rome at the cross, but according to Paul, that rejection and defeat were overturned, and Jesus was vindicated by God. Jesus was right; Caesar was wrong. Here's how the hymn says it:

Therefore God exalted him even more highly
and gave him the name
that is above every other name,
so that at the name given to Jesus
every knee should bend,
in heaven and on earth and under the earth,
and every tongue should confess
that Jesus Christ is Lord,
to the glory of God the Father.

(Philippians 2:9-11)

The problem in Paul's world is that there was a lord's name that required obedience and obeisance: Caesar. The question that emerged is a dangerous one: Who is the actual, real Lord? Who has the right and authority to rule the world? To whom do we bend our knee in honor and reverence? The conflict of the Christmas story deepens when we hear this challenge.

Savior

As we saw in the Priene Calendar Inscription, Augustus was understood to be a gift of providence, bestowed upon the world as a savior of sorts. For many Christians, the idea of a savior is analogous to one who forgives sins. However, in the ancient world, to be a savior was to be a liberator, a deliverer, a rescuer from harm or danger.

Remember, after the assassination of Julius Caesar, Rome was thrown into total chaos. The fabric of the Republic was being torn apart, and Augustus's victory in the civil wars that followed brought a renewed stability that Rome desperately needed. To proclaim Augustus as savior meant that he had delivered Rome from what seemed like certain destruction. This understanding of the savior is reflected in the words of Paulus Fabius Maximus, the governor of Roman Asia Minor, who suggested recalibrating the calendar around Augustus's birth. Notice the language:

> [Augustus] restored order when everything was disintegrating and falling into chaos and gave a new look to the whole world, a world which would have met destruction with the utmost pleasure if Caesar had not been born as a common blessing to all.[3]

If not for Caesar, he argued, not just Rome, but the whole world itself would have been destroyed. Caesar's birth was a gift to the world because he saved the world from doom. Who else could claim such an accomplishment?

Both Matthew and Luke employ this language, not in reference to Caesar, but to Jesus. We saw in Luke 2 that his angels announced to the shepherds the birth of a savior who is also the promised Messiah. In Matthew, savior language occurs in Joseph's dream after learning of Mary's unusual pregnancy. Joseph intended to divorce Mary quietly, but in a dream, an angel explained how important this birth would be:

> *"Joseph, son of David, do not be afraid to take Mary as your wife, for the child conceived in her is from the Holy Spirit. She will bear a son, and you are to name him Jesus, for he will save his people from their sins."*
>
> *(Matthew 1:20-21)*

Again, if we hear only "forgiveness" when the angel says "save," we miss the larger claim: Jesus, not Caesar, is what a true liberator, deliverer, rescuer—the Savior—looks like. Embedded within Christmas stories in Luke and Matthew is the radical claim that Jesus is the true Son of God and Savior of the world.

Bringer of Peace

Central to Roman imperial theology was the conviction that Augustus had brought peace on earth. In his own monumental inscription, the Res Gestae Divi Augusti, or the Deeds of the Divine Augustus, Augustus claims to be Rome's peace-bringer. In the following excerpt, he references the gateway of Janus, a temple in Rome that featured doors that would remain open when Rome was at war and would be shut only during times of peace. Augustus claimed that he shut those doors more times during his reign than in the entirety of Roman history before him:

> It was the will of our ancestors that the gateway of Janus Quirinus should be shut when victories had secured peace by land and sea throughout the whole empire of the Roman people; from the foundation of the city down to my birth, tradition records that it was shut only twice, but while I was the leading citizen the senate resolved that it should be shut on three occasions.[4]

Augustus is credited with ushering in the Pax Romana, or Roman peace, a period of just over two hundred years of unprecedented political and economic stability, marked by peace and security across the empire. The key is that this stability was made possible by Roman strength and military might. To put it another way, peace was achieved by Rome's defeat of its enemies, often through the exercise of violence against defiant people and populations.

In his work, *Agricola*, the historian Tacitus records a speech by Calgacus, a leader of the tribes in northern Britain, just before war with Rome in 83 CE. Calgacus described the Pax Romana in less than flattering terms:

> These plunderers of the world, after exhausting the land by their devastations, are rifling the ocean: stimulated by avarice, if their enemy be rich; by ambition, if poor; unsatiated by the East and by the West: the only people who behold wealth and indigence with equal avidity. To ravage, to slaughter, to usurp under false titles, they call empire; and where they make a desert, they call it peace.[5]

Roman peace was for Romans, and it came at the expense of whoever stood in Rome's way. The Christmas stories announce a different kind of peace on earth, a peace that is embodied not in the violence of empire, but in the innocence and vulnerability of a child born on the margins of power. Jesus's way of bringing peace would stand in stark relief to that of Rome's:

- Jesus did not seek to hoard wealth and power. He regularly taught his listeners to share and even give away their wealth. He embodied that teaching by feeding the hungry and uplifting the forgotten, oppressed, and marginalized.
- Jesus also did not engage in violence to bring about some watered-down version of peace. Instead, he taught his followers to love their enemies, to turn the other cheek, and to enact justice on earth, as it is in heaven.

- Jesus did not respond to his Roman executioners with hatred but instead prayed for their forgiveness.

Proclaiming Jesus as the bringer of peace on earth was a radical challenge to the empire's message and propaganda. Jesus and Caesar offered diametrically opposed visions and employed drastically different means. Whose way of bringing peace was better? Whose vision was inspired by God/the gods? How would peace ultimately be made on earth? These are the questions embedded in the Christmas stories.

Gospel

The word gospel comes to us from the Greek word *euangelion*. It's a combination of the word good (*eu*) and the word for message or announcement (*angelion*). A gospel is an announcement of a good message or good news. Christians know this word well, don't we? When we hear it, we might even think about it as a list of things we need to believe about Jesus. However, that is not how the word was first understood. *Euangelion* was not solely a theological idea; rather, it was deeply intertwined with politics. A "gospel" was an announcement of something good that had happened in the empire, usually related to some victory of the emperor. Did Rome win a war? The announcement was used to proclaim good news. Was a new ruler born, or had a new leader risen to power? Good news. In many ways, it was a kind of propaganda meant to cast the emperor in the roles we have already explored: savior and bringer of peace. That's exactly how the Priene Calendar Inscription uses the idea: "Caesar, who by his epiphany exceeded the hopes of those who prophesied good tidings . . . the birthday of the god first brought to the world the good tidings residing in him."[6] The good news lived in Augustus, and he embodied it through the wars he fought and the enemies he conquered. Peacemaking in the empire was a bloody endeavor.

By contrast, Jesus's gospel was announced as good news for the poor. It centered on the accessibility and availability of God's kingdom—not somewhere else, someday else, for someone else, but as a present reality, right here and now. In the first words spoken by Jesus in Mark's Gospel, we are invited into the core, the heartbeat of his vision: "The time is fulfilled, and the kingdom of God has come near; repent, and believe in the good news" (Mark 1:15).

Notice that this kingdom is not announced as arriving through victory over an enemy, but as already present, perhaps buried in the ground like seeds just awaiting some water and care. Jesus and Caesar Augustus had two significantly different gospels, resulting in two vastly different outcomes. Caesar benefited Rome as an empire, with the primary beneficiaries being Caesar himself and the people in his orbit. Isn't that how empires have always worked? Let just enough trickle down to keep the average citizen from becoming too restless, but the lion's share, and then some, pools at the top. Jesus's vision benefited everyone. It was food in the bellies of the hungry, healing for the sick, community for the excluded, and an opportunity for those who had been on the wrong side of history to change their hearts and minds so that they could be part of the dream of God unfolding in the world. This vision was not about retribution; it was a restorative justice that made space for everyone to belong. That is real, actual good news—a real gospel!

Light

The story of Jesus is replete with references to light. Jesus is the "true light, which enlightens everyone" come into the world (John 1:9). He was also the "light of the world" (John 8:12; 9:5). He was a "great light" seen by a people in darkness (Matthew 4:16). According to Simeon, he was also a "light for revelation to the gentiles" (Luke 2:32). And Jesus said his followers themselves would also be "the light of the world" (Matthew 5:14).

It might be surprising to learn that a similar image of light was present in the birth myth of Caesar Augustus. According to the Roman historian Suetonius, Augustus was actually the product of a divine–human union between his mother, Atia, and the Roman solar god, Apollo. One of the signs that accompanied his birth was a dream his father, also Octavius, had. In that dream, a sunbeam issued forth from Atia's womb, confirming that he was a child of Apollo.

Who, then, is bringing light into the world? The true light that casts out the darkness of war and fear? The light that has the potential to usher in an unprecedented "golden age" for the world? That is another question that these Christmas stories ask us to ponder.

While these stories of Augustus's birth emerged after Jesus was born, remember that the stories about Jesus's life were all written at the earliest forty and at the latest eighty years after the events. Would the authors of the Gospels, aware of the Roman propaganda, intentionally choose language and themes that explore the conflict and challenge between these two figures and their different visions? It doesn't seem that far-fetched, does it?

NARRATIVE, COUNTERNARRATIVE, AND RESISTANCE

While this chapter may have felt so far like a deep dive or drinking from a fire hose, in reality, we have just skimmed the surface of the connections and challenges between these two competing visions that collide in the Christmas stories. I hope it has become evident that the context in which Jesus was born is not merely background noise. It is the reality in which he lived and worked and the reality that shaped his vision and response.

Empires always construct a narrative. That narrative, it just so happens, almost always benefits and protects the empire's power, stability, and control. You can crucify a lot of people if they are deemed a threat to national security, after all. Thankfully, in both the past and present, the narrative of the empire is not the only story being told.

In the Christmas stories, we are offered a counternarrative that rejects the claims of Caesar and Rome and paints for us a different possible future. The Jesus movement began as an alternative to the vision of empire, and despite all the ways his movement has been co-opted by countless empires over the millennia, that radical challenge can still be heard in these stories if we listen for it.

Advent and Christmas are not just seasons of sentimentality; they are also seasons for cultivating resistance. In some ways, the world is totally different today than it was during the lives of Jesus and Augustus. We have gained a lot of information and experience and have made immeasurable advances in science, medicine, and our understanding of humanity. Yet, in so many ways, the world is tragically the same. The world is still violent, inequities abound, and the poor are still waiting for the good news to arrive for them. As a species, we have embraced Caesar's understanding of peace at the expense of our own flourishing. Justice is delayed, and as we know, that means it has been denied for so many. How can the season of Advent prepare us to resist the brutality and injustice that crowd the pages of our history books and play out live across our television screens and social media feeds? Let's briefly consider the themes of Advent and how this season can do just that.

HOPE

Advent begins with a focus on hope, but not an esoteric wishful thinking. It's a specific hope that the world we imagine and envision is not grounded in naiveté or baseless optimism. In the Jewish tradition that formed Jesus, particularly in the words of the prophets, this hope for a different kind of future is vibrant. Many prophets dreamed out loud about a world of peace and prosperity that was not produced by violence and injustice but was the consequence of a nonviolent world of fairness and equity. Those same longings are present in the teaching and actions of Jesus. Gathering a diverse crowd around the table, teaching them to share their resources with one another, and everyone receiving enough was not just about lunch; it was both a dress rehearsal for that other world and a recipe for making it so.

Some days hope does feel a bit silly, doesn't it? After all, the Jesus movement has existed for 2,000 years, and we are still dealing with the same old problems that he faced. I understand that feeling, and the immensity of the world's problems can feel overwhelming most days. In times like that, I am reminded of something G. K. Chesterton once wrote: "The Christian ideal has not been tried and found wanting; it has been found difficult and left untried."[7] Doesn't that feel true at the deepest level? Can't you feel that in your bones? We have not yet fully leaned into what Jesus envisioned, have we? Can you imagine what might be possible if we did?

Perhaps it would be helpful to reimagine and reframe what we mean by hope. It is not simply a wish or desire. Hope is an action. So, too, with hope's sibling, waiting. Advent hope is a hope that waits with both resilience and action. But how, you might be asking, can waiting be active? What does that even look like? With a family as big as mine (there are seven of us), you won't be surprised to know that it can be hard to find common ground on things like what to eat for dinner or what movie to watch during our family nights.

One thing we agree on wholeheartedly is that we all love, and I mean love, the beach. We love the ocean, the way a beach town smells and feels, and especially the food. Every year, we try to find ourselves oceanside for a few days to just enjoy our favorite environment. There's one problem, however. The nearest beach to us is almost eight hours away. It takes what feels like forever, especially to the kids, for us to get our toes in the sand. We could let that stop us, but we don't. We load up the car, point it south, and we start taking the trip one mile at a time. We have to wait, sure, but we don't wait at home hoping the beach will come to us. We wait in the car as we move toward our goal minute by minute.

This is the kind of waiting that Advent invites us to participate in. The waiting that knows we can't just make the world a more just and generous place at the snap of our fingers but that trusts deeply that, together with God, we can move toward that vision day by day. For both Christmas past and Christmas present, the Caesars and would-be Caesars of the world will try to snuff out our hope and our will to actively wait. The invitation of the Christmas story is to see the bigger picture and to trust that, as we do what we can in this moment, together, God will join us in the work of making the world better for everyone. Advent also invites us to resist the false peace that the empire sells us. Recently, I was scrolling through my social media feed and noticed a post from the U.S. Department of Defense. The post was video-based with text superimposed over the changing background. The images were of tanks and bombers, and the text came from Matthew 5, the Sermon on the Mount. Specifically, it was one of the Beatitudes:

> *"Blessed are the peacemakers, for they will be called children of God."*
> *(Matthew 5:9)*

As we've seen, this same sentiment of peace through power is embedded in Caesar's propaganda, which held that peace could come only through strength and victory: We make peace when we dominate our enemies. Jesus offered a dramatically different vision, one that insists that peace is made not through victory but through justice—a justice, in the vision of the prophet Micah, that means everyone has access to the necessities of life and can live in security, free from fear (Micah 4:4). I think often of the protest refrain that must be chanted far too often that succinctly names this reality: "No justice. No peace." That was never a threat, but always an acknowledgment that when the world is just and fair, when everyone has enough and can live without fear and with stability, peace becomes real and possible. This is the vision we find throughout the Hebrew Prophets: swords beaten into plowshares, a banquet with room for everyone, each person having access to the means of sustainability. Advent resists the false, cheap peace and helps us build the spiritual muscle to be peacemakers in the way of Jesus. Another theme of Advent is joy. Do you ever feel guilty about feeling joy? In light of the suffering and pain of the world, how can we possibly feel good about experiencing joy when everything is, well, kind of a mess? Enter the brilliance of the poet Mary Oliver. In her poem "Don't Hesitate," she both names this pervasive sense of guilt we often feel over experiencing joy and calls us to embrace the gift of joy when it comes to us. She writes about all the problems and pains of the world as reasons to make space for joy. "If you suddenly and unexpectedly feel joy, don't hesitate. . . . Joy is not made to be a crumb."[8]

But wait, isn't that why we should suppress our joy, because of the calamity and pain of the world? No, Oliver says, joy is a way of pushing back against the pain and injustice of the world. This idea of joy as a kind of resistance can be found right in the middle of the Christmas stories. The angels appear to some shepherds and announce good news of great joy—complete with an enthusiastic, celebratory song—in the middle of the night and, more importantly, in the context of the Roman occupation of Judea. Neither the angels nor the shepherds hedged or muted their joy. The angels filled the night sky with song, and the shepherds returned from visiting the Holy Family joyfully praising God for the experience.

Joy resists the cynicism, despair, and resignation that the powerful count on to limit our capacity to resist their unjust ordering of the world. Joy is not to be feared or avoided but taken in and embraced with both arms. After all, "Joy is not made to be a crumb."[9]

Finally, Advent calls us to the path of love. In all things—our celebration and joy, and our resistance and struggle—love is the means and the end of our work. Some Christians have decided that the ends justify the means, so any actions required to bring about their desired ends are simply compromises that must be made.

This is not the way of Jesus, friends. For Jesus, even our resistance is an act of love, not only for the oppressed and marginalized, but also for the oppressors of the world. This is, after all, good news of great joy for all people, right? Love is not just a sentimental feeling, but a concrete action. We resist in love to help those in need, and we resist in love to call those doing harm to realize that they are violating both the humanity of their victims and their own.

Social media has surely made this more difficult, even for well-meaning people. Behind a keyboard, it is far easier to be mean, dismissive, and to say things you'd never actually say face-to-face to another person. As a person with a natural proclivity for sarcasm, I have too often succumbed to this kind of approach. The problem is that it doesn't change anyone's mind and only deepens the divide between us. It is possible to name the harm and call those perpetuating it to do better without returning the harm to them. Love calls us to seek the well-being of everyone, and in doing so to show up in a way that embodies the ethic of Jesus.

JESUS AND CAESAR TODAY

The Christmas stories leave us with some questions that, on the surface, seem to be easy to answer. Yet, living out the implications of those answers in our everyday lives is a challenge. Can we do it? Jesus seemed to believe that with God's help, and one another, it could really happen on earth, as it is in heaven. Let's close this chapter by reflecting on some of these important questions:

- Whose vision is better for the world, Jesus or Caesar?
- Who is really Lord? If Jesus is, then Caesar isn't, and vice versa.
- Who is the bringer of actual, lasting peace? If Jesus is the Prince of Peace, then we can't pretend that what Caesar masquerades as peace is good for the world.
- Who is our savior? Who is bringing real liberation, deliverance, and rescue?
- Finally, who is the true light of the world? In whose light will we stand for illumination and warmth?

Christmas insists that, if we want to embrace the good news of Jesus, then we must also reject the false gospel of Caesar. When Christians grapple with these challenging and meaningful questions, Christmas and Advent become seasons that can empower us to change the world.

CHAPTER 2

WHAT'S IN A (LIST OF) NAMES?

CHAPTER 2

What's in a (List of) Names?

FAMILY TREES

A couple of years ago, I developed a sudden interest in my family tree. Up until that point, I had never in my four decades of life thought much about past generations of my family beyond those that were familiar to me. I knew who my great-grandparents were. I was fortunate to spend time with a few of them when I was smaller, but beyond that, I hadn't been very curious. That all changed when my wife learned a bit about her family history, and it sparked that wonder in me: I knew where I came from, but now I wanted to know from whom.

To begin that quest, I created an Ancestry.com account and started piecing together the branches that comprise my family tree. I saw names and even faces that were unknown to me, but at the same time, they were deeply a part of who I am and who I am becoming. It was both a humbling and grounding experience. It gifted me with a new sense of belonging and connection that I had not previously known. My hope is to one day fill in the still unknown branches of my family tree, giving names and gratitude to the generations that made my life possible. To others, it's just a list, but to me, it explains from where I came and, in some ways, shapes where I am going.

The Bible contains many similar lists—we call them genealogies—and they can be less than riveting to read. Many Christians, when they arrive at a list of "begats and begets" in books like Genesis, Numbers, or Chronicles, just skip right over those names. They can feel a bit like someone showing you slides of their vacation, can't they? The people involved might find it all interesting, but the rest of us would rather just move on. We tend to zone out the parts that don't feel as inspiring or personally relevant.

Take, for example, the list of Adam's descendants in Genesis 5:3-8:

> *When Adam had lived one hundred thirty years, he became the father of a son in his likeness, according to his image, and named him Seth. The days of Adam after he became the father of Seth were eight hundred years, and he had other sons and daughters. Thus all the days that Adam lived were nine hundred thirty years, and he died.*
>
> *When Seth had lived one hundred five years, he became the father of Enosh. Seth lived after the birth of Enosh eight hundred seven years and had other sons and daughters. Thus all the days of Seth were nine hundred twelve years, and he died.*

It just keeps going for the rest of the chapter. How does this short snippet strike you? Does it feel compelling? Relevant? Will it impact your life or your faith in meaningful ways? Would you rather watch paint dry? I totally get it. Reading the names of who was whose father doesn't typically feel like an inspirational, transformative experience.

That's why the way Matthew begins his Gospel is so . . . strange, at least on the surface. While, as we've seen, Matthew is not the earliest of the Gospels to be written, it does have the distinct privilege of being first in the order of the New Testament books. Matthew is the leadoff hitter for the New Testament—he offers first-time readers of the Bible an introductory portrait of Jesus and his life. That being the case, how he begins his narrative is kind of a big deal.

When I was doing my undergraduate degree in English with an emphasis on writing, my teachers ingrained in me the importance of the opening paragraphs in catching and holding the reader's attention. It's called a hook, and it is crucial to have a good one if you want readers to get beyond the opening lines of your writing. After all, as the band Blues Traveler taught us in the 90s, "it's the hook that brings you back."[1]

What, then, is Matthew's hook? How does he open his story of Jesus in the most compelling way possible to draw in his readers so he can unfold for them the most important story that he could ever possibly tell? If you are unfamiliar with Matthew's Gospel, you may think I am making this up, but I assure you, I am not: Matthew begins with a genealogy. Talk about the opposite of a hook. I bet you might have even yawned just reading that last sentence.

That stands in stark contrast to Mark, which Matthew used as a major source for his own story. Mark launches into his narrative right away with John the Baptist preaching in the wilderness, preparing the way for Jesus. One feature of Mark's literary style is fast-paced storytelling. Think action movie—quick cuts, no time wasted. Matthew chooses a different path. While he had no idea he was crafting the opening lines of something that would be called the "New Testament," he begins, with no introductory remarks as to why, with a list of Jesus's ancestors.

> *An account of the genealogy of Jesus the Messiah, the son of David, the son of Abraham.*
>
> *(Matthew 1:1)*

What follows are sixteen more verses that trace the origin of Jesus from Abraham, through David and the Exile, to his birth to Joseph and Mary. Those seventeen total verses have been referred to as the "most boring verses in the entire Bible."[2] Quite the choice for the opening words of this Gospel and the New Testament as a whole. In fact, the very presence of this opening who's who of Jesus's family tree might be surprising for many readers of the Gospel. They are never recited in Christmas pageants and rarely sermonized about in churches. We move over it, perhaps not even noticing, to get to the birth story that Matthew narrates.

Before we write these seventeen verses off and skip ahead to the Nativity stories proper, I want to pause and ask the question: Why did Matthew choose this seemingly boring introduction when he had examples (Mark) of the opposite? Why not just launch into the good part? The answer might surprise us and change how we view this genealogy.

A TALE OF TWO GENEALOGIES

Before we attempt to uncover a possible explanation for Matthew's decision to begin with Jesus's family tree, I first want to acknowledge that this is not the only version of Jesus's genealogy in the New Testament. The other is found in the third chapter of the Gospel of Luke, and it is surprisingly different from Matthew's in several ways. Those differences are fascinating because Matthew wrote some ten or more years before Luke, and it is very possible that Luke had not just Mark, but also Matthew as a source for his Gospel. These differences are key because they reflect each writer's agenda and give us helpful insight into what the writer hopes we will learn, especially in Matthew. So, hang with me as we explore these differences, because they are key to understanding how genealogies were used in the ancient world. It's quite different than what we think of today.

First, while Matthew begins his story with Jesus's lineage, Luke waits until after Jesus's baptism to offer his list. Another interesting divergence is that these two lists are in opposite chronological order. Matthew begins with Abraham and traces his lineage to Jesus, while Luke begins with Jesus and traces his line all the way back to Adam, the first human in the narrative of Genesis 2. While Matthew grounds Jesus firmly in the Jewish tradition, as the son of David, Luke expands beyond the vision, showing Jesus to be the son of both God and humanity.

Further, these two writers offer a different number of generations between Jesus and Abraham, and while there are some agreements between them about members of Jesus's ancestry, there is also significant disagreement. Joseph is identified as the son of Jacob in Matthew's genealogy but as the son of Heli in Luke's. If we keep going back in time, there are other discrepancies, but two key figures, Abraham and David, appear in and are central to both versions.

The structure of these genealogies is also different. Matthew's genealogy is structured around three groups of generations, the first two containing fourteen generations and the last with thirteen—from Abraham to David, from David to the Exile, and from the Exile to Jesus. Forty-two generations in total, although he only lists forty-one names (David appears twice). It is likely that the number fourteen, repeated three times in this genealogy, is also evoking the memory of David, because the characters of the name in Hebrew add up to the number fourteen in gematria.[3] Luke, on the other hand, lists a total of seventy-seven names between Jesus and Adam, with fifty-six of those names occurring between Jesus and Abraham.

Why do I raise these differences? While I love a good Bible-nerd conversation, this goes a bit deeper, into the heart of what a genealogy was in the ancient world. As I began this chapter, I shared my experience exploring my ancestry and how it helped me feel more connected to my ancestors—I found marriage licenses and court records that gave me a concrete connection to the names that populate the branches of my family tree. That is not what ancient genealogies were trying to do. It was just the opposite. Ancient genealogies were about the destiny of the person being rooted in a particular family. They were almost always created in hindsight, meaning that a life so well lived or that made an outsized impact could only be explained by casting that figure into a family tree alongside figures of the past who were revered for their accomplishments. An example from outside the Bible might help clarify this point.

Julius Caesar and Caesar Augustus are two figures whose lives impacted the story of Jesus, one indirectly and the other directly, and their story will bring into focus how genealogies were used in the ancient world. Just months before his death in 44 BCE, Julius Caesar rewrote his will, naming his grandnephew Octavian as his adoptive son and principal heir. This was significant because the Julian family, to which Julius Caesar belonged, claimed descent from Aeneas, a Trojan hero who fled to Italy after Troy fell. Aeneas was the ancestor of the Romans and was said to be the son of the goddess of love, Venus. This connection made the Julian line divine—they were the sons of gods. This lineage is preserved in the *Aeneid*, a work by the poet Virgil that became Rome's great national epic. In a scene set in the underworld, Aeneas is talking to Anchises, his father, who shows him a procession of future Roman leaders, culminating with Caesar Augustus—the exalted name conferred on Octavian upon his ascension to the throne as the first Roman emperor. Virgil writes:

> Here is Caesar, who will one day bring peace to the world
> And impose his law on proud peoples far and wide;
> He will be born of the line of Julus,
> Descended from great Aeneas by royal bloodline;
> His reign will open a golden age for Rome and the world.[4]

This brief genealogy situates Augustus in the line of Rome's founders, themselves the product of a divine-human relationship. The meaning could not be missed: Augustus was the direct descendant of the gods, and his was the right to rule the world and lead Rome into a "golden age." Here's the rub: Virgil wrote these lines after Augustus had become Rome's unquestioned ruler. He was not predicting history but using the past to explain how on earth someone unexpected like Augustus could find himself at the steering wheel of the known world.

It is so important to remember that the writers of the Bible were part of this ancient world and the conventions that shaped it. When they put pen to papyrus to tell their stories of Jesus, they did not sever all ties with the cultural matrix that had shaped them. It was the exact opposite. They were co-opting that matrix to tell the story of another king, one with a greater royal bloodline, who would really open the path to a golden age of peace on earth. Genealogy was always destiny in the ancient world; the past was meant to substantiate the present and shape the future. Keeping all this in mind, let's return to Matthew's genealogy and look for clues that help us understand how he is leveraging Israel's past as the launchpad for the story of Jesus.

SON OF ABRAHAM, SON OF DAVID

Matthew doesn't make us wait very long before he lays his cards on the table. In fact, he lets the cat out of the bag in the opening verse of his Gospel:

> *An account of the genealogy of Jesus the Messiah, the son of David, the son of Abraham.*
>
> *(Matthew 1:1)*

While he will go on to name-drop other significant figures of Israel's past, like Solomon, Hezekiah, and Josiah, who were all significant kings in Judah's history, the first two Matthew mentions are central to the picture of Jesus he wants to frame for his readers. Jesus is both the son of David and the son of Abraham. Let's explore the significance of both of these ancestors of Jesus, beginning with the first in chronological order, Abraham.

When we first meet Abraham, he's known as Abram, a name meaning "exalted father." Oh, the tragic irony of that name. Abram and his wife Sarai (later, Sarah) were unable to have children, and when we first meet them, they are already past their child-rearing prime. Abram was in his mid-seventies, and Sarai was a decade younger—not usually the stage of life in which one shops for cribs and diaper genies.

We meet Abram in Genesis 12, right after a brief genealogy of his family in chapter 11, and the action begins immediately. God speaks to Abram and calls him to leave behind his home and his family, everything and everyone he has known, and to head out for "the land that I will show you" (Genesis 12:1). Abram is not given the entire plan. There is no address that he can input to get turn-by-turn directions for the journey ahead. Yet, he does just as God tells him . . . sort of. He takes his nephew Lot along, a decision that will lead to some trouble later in the story. The point of this journey, God tells Abram, is for him to become "a great nation." If Abram is faithful to obey, God will bless and multiply his family beyond his wildest imagination. This blessing is not exclusive, however, but it is instrumental. God will bless Abram and his descendants so that through them God will bless the entire human family. That meaning is reflected in the change of name Abram receives from God in Genesis 17:

> *No longer shall your name be Abram, but your name shall be Abraham, for I have made you the ancestor of a multitude of nations.*
>
> (Genesis 17:5)

The promise Abram receives is that he will not be just an exalted father, but the ancestor of nations. That must have felt impossible for Abraham to believe, as he was now ninety-nine years old and his wife was pushing ninety, but he did. He trusted this promise and arranged his life accordingly. To be sure, the story does not unfold without fits and starts. There is no lack of mistakes, missteps, and drama. Abraham doesn't always make the right decisions, but who among us does? He would, however, become the gold-standard example of true faithfulness—understood as trust—in the unfolding story of Israel:

> *And [Abram] believed the* LORD, *and the* LORD *reckoned it to him as righteousness.*
>
> (Genesis 15:6)

It should not surprise us, then, that Abraham, the bastion of faith in and faithfulness to God, would be at the front of mind for the writers who composed the letters and Gospels that comprise our New Testament. Jesus, they believed, was a true son of Abraham because he embodied the same trust in God as Abraham. If you recall, Matthew wrote his Jesus story in the 80s of the first century of our common era. Paul wrote some thirty years before Matthew penned his opening verse, and Paul was already making the connection between Jesus and Abraham.

There are many places we could turn to for an example of this connection in Paul's writings, but two specific passages are helpful for understanding how Paul made the connection between the story of Abraham and the life of Jesus. The first is from Galatians, one of his earliest letters, written sometime in the late 40s to early 50s, and the second is from Romans, one of his latest letters, likely written in the late 50s to early 60s. At the bookends of his ministry, Paul wrote to these two communities that were dealing with similar challenges about the significance of the story of Abraham as an interpretive lens for the life of Jesus.

Both the churches in Galatia and Rome were dealing with internal conflicts about how Jewish followers of Jesus and Gentile followers of Jesus should relate to one another. Should there be a separation between them? Can Gentiles embrace the story of Jesus without first also embracing a conversion to a Jewish identity? Many Jewish followers of Jesus, including those representing James and the Jerusalem church, disagreed with Paul's conclusion that Gentiles need not convert first before following Jesus. That was the message Paul would preach in the communities he visited, but that teaching was regularly met with strong resistance. This shows up in letters like Galatians and even the Corinthian correspondence—Paul would preach and teach in a community, leave to go elsewhere, and then a group of counterapostles would arrive and tell the community that Paul's ideas were rubbish and unfounded. This seemed to cause at least some members of these communities to either reconsider Paul's message or perhaps abandon it altogether. Inevitably, word would get back to Paul about the confusion, and he would sit down and dictate a letter speaking to those concerns. That is the exact purpose of Galatians: to counterattack the argument of those who sought to undermine Paul's message.

How does Paul do this? By referring to the promise God made to Abraham in Genesis 15, that his blessing was instrumental, not exclusive. Abraham and his descendants would be a channel of blessing even for the Gentiles.

> *Just as Abraham "believed God, and it was reckoned to him as righteousness," so, you see, those who believe are the descendants of Abraham. And the scripture, foreseeing that God would reckon as righteous the gentiles by faith, declared the gospel beforehand to Abraham, saying, "All the gentiles shall be blessed in you." For this reason, those who believe are blessed with Abraham who believed.*
>
> (*Galatians 3:6-9*)

Gentiles, Paul argues, have always been on the periphery of the blessing promised to Abraham, but in the story and person of Jesus, that implicit connection becomes explicit. He continues with an innovative interpretation, we might even call it a kind of negotiation, with the text. He references the promise to Abraham that his "offspring" would receive the benefit of this covenant, but Paul makes an interpretive move that makes the offspring not a people, but a specific person.

> *Now the promises were made to Abraham and to his offspring; it does not say, "And to offsprings," as of many, but it says, "And to your offspring," that is, to one person, who is Christ.*
>
> (*Galatians 3:16*)

For Paul, the promise made to Abraham was brought into fullness in the person of Jesus. The blessing and inclusion of all nations were happening in and through the Jesus movement. That led Paul to an interesting and surprising (in his context) claim about the equality of all people in this Jesus movement.

> *. . . for in Christ Jesus you are all children of God through faith. As many of you as were baptized into Christ have clothed yourselves with Christ. There is no longer Jew or Greek; there is no longer slave or free; there is no longer male and female, for all of you are one in Christ Jesus. And if you belong to Christ, then you are Abraham's offspring, heirs according to the promise.*
> *(Galatians 3:26-29)*

The solution to the conflict in Galatia, Paul asserts, is to understand that the story of Jesus is the fulfillment of God's promises to Abraham and, by extension, the whole world. Gentiles, in Paul's mind, could become part of Abraham's family tree in the same way that Abraham himself became the "father of many nations," through faith in this promise.

A second key letter for understanding how the memory of Abraham shaped Paul's understanding of Jesus can be found in Romans. In chapter 4, Paul argues that God's promise to Abraham preceded the giving of the Law, which for him means that this promise was universal in scope from the beginning.

> *For what does the scripture say? "Abraham believed God, and it was reckoned to him as righteousness."*
> *(Romans 4:3)*

> *For the promise that he would inherit the world did not come to Abraham or to his descendants through the law but through the righteousness of faith.*
> *(Romans 4:13)*

We must be cautious in what we do with Paul's words here. Paul was himself Jewish, and I am convinced he never saw himself as anything but Jewish. He had no intention of starting or converting to a new religion. He believed deeply, as did Jesus, that he was living at the "end of the age," at a time of great possibility and also great danger. The world as he knew it, he believed, was soon going to come to an end. A new age would dawn, and for Paul, that new age should be marked by a new kind of human community that transcended the hierarchical ways in which humans have always carved up the world. So, as Paul writes to the Romans, a community he did not found and did not seem to know well, he wants to solidify the bonds between the Jewish and Gentile community members by appealing to the story of Abraham and insisting that something larger was going on.

That connection between Jesus and Abraham would continue to be developed in the writings of the New Testament. As we saw in the Introduction, in John's Gospel, Jesus and his opponents have tense conversations about what it means to be a "child of Abraham." For Paul, to be the "son of Abraham" meant that Jesus was the fulfillment, the embodiment, of Abrahamic faithfulness.

The second of the pivotal figures Matthew mentions before even listing the ancestors of Jesus is David, the shepherd boy, the slayer of the giant, and depicted as the uniter of the tribes of Israel and Judah into a flourishing kingdom. In the books of Samuel, David is presented as an unlikely figure to become the king of Israel. He was the youngest of his family, only an afterthought when the prophet Samuel came calling. God had told Samuel that the first king Israel had known, Saul, had been rejected by God. Samuel was then sent to Bethlehem in Judah, to the house of a man named Jesse, the grandson of Boaz and Ruth, to search for Saul's replacement. The story unfolds dramatically. One by one, Jesse's sons appear before Samuel, each one more impressive than the last, but each one rejected by God—all seven. Then David was called in from tending the family flock in the fields, and immediately Samuel knew that this was God's anointed. Eventually, David would receive a promise from God that his dynasty would never end, with the caveat that his descendants' faithfulness to God would ultimately determine the success or failure of the kingdom. In 2 Samuel 7, the prophet Nathan spoke to David on God's behalf:

> *Thus says the LORD of hosts: I took you from the pasture, from following the sheep to be prince over my people Israel, and I have been with you wherever you went and have cut off all your enemies from before you, and I will make for you a great name, like the name of the great ones of the earth. And I will appoint a place for my people Israel and will plant them, so that they may live in their own place and be disturbed no more, and evildoers shall afflict them no more, as formerly, from the time that I appointed judges over my people Israel, and I will give you rest from all your enemies. Moreover, the LORD declares to you that the LORD will make you a house. When your days are fulfilled and you lie down with your ancestors, I will raise up your offspring after you, who shall come forth from your body, and I will establish his kingdom. He shall build a house for my name, and I will establish the throne of his kingdom forever. I will be a father to him, and he shall be a son to me. When he commits iniquity, I will punish him with a rod such as mortals use, with blows inflicted by human beings. But I will not take my steadfast love from him, as I took it from Saul, whom I put away from before you. Your house and your kingdom shall be made sure forever before me; your throne shall be established forever.*
>
> *(2 Samuel 7:8-16)*

By Jesus's day, those words likely brought more sting than comfort. The promised Davidic dynasty lay in ruins. The United Kingdom only lasted for one more generation. Upon the death of Solomon and the ascension of his son Rehoboam, the kingdom was torn in two. Israel was the more powerful and dominant kingdom to the north, but David's line would rule in Judah, the smaller and weaker Southern Kingdom. That status as the younger, weaker sibling was actually somewhat beneficial. When Israel was destroyed and exiled by the brutal Assyrian Empire in 722 BCE, Judah remained. Eventually, the Judahite kingdom became a vassal to Assyria and then Babylon, being forced to pay tribute, but they also continued to enjoy a modicum of self-governance. That would all change in the most devastating of ways.

Around 601 BCE, the king of Judah, Jehoiakim, with the encouragement of Egypt, rebelled against the Babylonians, led by King Nebuchadnezzar. This action led to a siege of Jerusalem. After Jehoiakim died, his son Jehoiachin became king, but soon thereafter surrendered himself and his administration to the Babylonians. They, along with the treasures of the Temple, were carried into exile in Babylon. In Jehoiachin's place, the Babylonians installed his uncle Mattaniah, whom they named Zedekiah, as the new client king of Judah. Even that was temporary, however.

Eleven years after his rise to the throne, Zedekiah also rebelled against the Babylonians. Second Kings 25 records the awful aftermath of that rebellion. Babylon came and razed the city, and they exiled the best and brightest of the people to Babylon. Zedekiah was captured, and the last thing he saw before the Babylonians gouged out his eyes was his own sons being executed. Zedekiah, the Davidic ruler now left without descendants, was taken into captivity in Babylon. The final scene of the books of Kings centers on Jehoiachin, still exiled in Babylon thirty-seven years later, being released from prison and dining at the table of King Evil-Merodach, Nebuchadnezzar's successor, for the remainder of his life.

Yet, even with the subsequent return from exile under the Persian Empire that followed, there was never the sense that "we're back." There was no Davidic king who returned to the throne to govern an independent Jewish kingdom. The promise from God to David was unfulfilled. That ache is reflected in the words of the Hebrew Prophets who envisioned a future in which promises made were translated into promises kept. Notice these words of longing for that once and future kingdom. Let's begin with Isaiah, who envisions the Davidic line as the stump of a tree, lopped off but sprouting with the possibility of new life.

> *A shoot shall come out from the stump of Jesse,*
> *and a branch shall grow out of his roots.*
> *The spirit of the LORD shall rest on him. . . .*
>
> *(Isaiah 11:1-2a)*

We also find in Jeremiah a similar vision of the rightful descendant of David ruling in justice and peace. The promise is not extinguished, says Jeremiah, just deferred.

> *The days are surely coming, says the LORD, when I will raise up for David a righteous Branch, and he shall reign as king and deal wisely and shall execute justice and righteousness in the land. In his days Judah will be saved, and Israel will live in safety.*
>
> *(Jeremiah 23:5-6a)*

Finally, in Ezekiel 37, we have a powerful prophetic image of a valley of dead, dry bones. God commands Ezekiel to prophesy to the bones, calling them back into spirit-infused life. This, God tells the prophet, is symbolic of what God intends for Israel as a whole. The Davidic kingdom would rise again:

> *Then he said to me, "Mortal, these bones are the whole house of Israel. They say, 'Our bones are dried up, and our hope is lost; we are cut off completely.' Therefore prophesy and say to them: Thus says the Lord GOD: I am going to open your graves and bring you up from your graves, O my people, and I will bring you back to the land of Israel. And you shall know that I am the LORD when I open your graves and bring you up from your graves, O my people. I will put my spirit within you, and you shall live, and I will place you on your own soil; then you shall know that I, the LORD, have spoken and will act, says the LORD."*
>
> *(Ezekiel 37:11-14)*

Calling Jesus the "son of David," here in Matthew's genealogy and the other Gospels, or earlier in Romans 1 by Paul, indicates that Jesus, as David's heir, is the rightful king of Israel. That means Caesar, who ruled Judea at the time, was an imposter. Thus, the first line that appears in the canonical order of the New Testament is an anti-empire statement. In a word, it was treason. Or, in the words of the late John Lewis, it's "good trouble."[5]

THE UNEXPECTED NAMES OF JESUS'S GENEALOGY

Ancient genealogies were somewhat predictable. They were, as we have seen, more about the destiny of the person being genealogized than about their literal, historical family line—it wasn't about biology or DNA; it was a way of explaining how a great person became great. These ancient genealogies were also usually patrilineal, meaning they were traced from male to male. Matthew's genealogy follows that somewhat predictable pattern, up to a point, but then it diverges in a surprising way: In addition to Mary, the mother of Jesus, Matthew names four other women, an unexpected occurrence in the ancient world. Let me briefly name them and give you an overview of their stories.

The first woman in Matthew's genealogy is Tamar, whose story is told in Genesis 38. She was married to Er, Judah's first-born—yes, that Judah, the son of Jacob from whom the Southern Kingdom of Judah took its name. When her husband Er died without children, the custom of levirate marriage required his brother to marry Tamar to continue the family line and provide for her, since widows often had no inheritance or protection. Onan, Er's brother, refused and died too, leaving only Shelah, Judah's youngest son. Judah, however, delayed, likely blaming Tamar for what had happened to his two sons. He sent her back to her father's house, supposedly until Shelah was grown.

Time passed, and Judah never followed through on his end of the bargain. Then Judah's wife died, and after the time of mourning for her, he set off for Timnah to shear his sheep. Knowing that Judah had no intention of fulfilling his duty to her, Tamar disguised herself as a prostitute and positioned herself on his route. Judah saw her but didn't recognize her. He secured her services by offering a kid from his flock as payment, but he left his signet ring, cord, and staff as collateral. More time passed, and Tamar discovered that she was pregnant.

When Judah learned of her pregnancy, he was incensed and ordered her execution, ignoring his own failure to act justly.

Tamar revealed the items, proving Judah was the father of her unborn child. Confronted with his own failure, Judah declared her to be more righteous than he was. Tamar gave birth to twins, one of them being Perez, an ancestor of Jesus.

The second woman named is Rahab. She was a prostitute who lived in the town of Jericho during the period of Joshua's conquest of Canaan. We are given nothing in the way of biography for her, but in all likelihood, she, too, was in a difficult situation, lacking the male protection required to survive a patriarchal society. In preparation for the battle for the city, Joshua, the Hebrew commander, sent two spies into the city on a reconnaissance mission. Their cover was quickly blown, and the king of Jericho began to search for the uninvited guests. When the search came to Rahab's house, she hid the Hebrew spies and protected them from being discovered by the king. Her only request was that her family be spared from the brutality that would visit Jericho. Joshua kept his word, and they spared Rahab and her family, who later settled in Israel. According to Matthew's genealogy, Rahab married a man named Salmon, and they had a son named Boaz.

That segues nicely into the third woman named in Matthew's genealogy, Ruth the Moabite. Her story is contained in the book named after her, and details how Ruth the Moabite—the Moabites were one of the most hated enemies of Israel—plays the heroine by saving both herself and her mother-in-law, Naomi. Naomi had moved with her husband and two sons from Bethlehem to Moab due to a famine. The irony is obvious in the original language: In the House of Bread (the meaning of Bethlehem), there was no bread to be found. Unfortunately, the story quickly goes from bad to worse. Naomi's husband dies not long after they arrived in Moab, and she was left with her two sons to make a life there. The two boys married Moabite women, but they too died, leaving Naomi and her two daughters-in-law, Ruth and Orpah, to fend for themselves. As we've seen, this context was not kind to women who had no male protection, so Naomi suggests the two women return to their families of origin to gain some semblance of provision and security. Orpah eventually agrees, but Ruth stays steadfastly committed to Naomi. In fact, she binds herself to her mother-in-law with some of the most beautiful and profound words in the entire Bible. I'll quote from the King James Version, because the poetry is likely familiar to us from weddings:

> *And Ruth said, Intreat me not to leave thee, or to return from following after thee: for whither thou goest, I will go; and where thou lodgest, I will lodge: thy people shall be my people, and thy God my God:*
>
> *Where thou diest, will I die, and there will I be buried: the LORD do so to me, and more also, if ought but death part thee and me.*
>
> *(Ruth 1:16-17, KJV)*

When they both returned to Bethlehem, Ruth took responsibility for the care and survival of Naomi. She eventually would catch the eye of Boaz, a relative of Naomi's husband. With Naomi's encouragement, Ruth eventually made her move. Taking the lead, she called on Boaz to marry her and fulfill his family obligation. There was only one tiny snag in her plan. Boaz was not the closest relative of Ruth's deceased husband. Like Tamar, the closest relative had no desire to fulfill his obligation to his relatives by marrying Ruth. That's when Boaz stepped in and fulfilled what had now become his responsibility to his family.

Boaz and Ruth married and had a son whom they named Obed, who in turn had a son named Jesse. Jesse then became the father of David. This means that David's great-grandmother was Ruth the Moabite, a vulnerable but courageous woman from a people that Israel hated, yet without her courageous action, we would never have had David, Solomon, or, according to Matthew, Jesus.

There are still two other women to be named, one implicitly and the other explicitly. First, we have a woman Matthew refers to only as "the wife of Uriah" (Matthew 1:6). Her name was Bathsheba. We meet her in 2 Samuel 11 and discover that she is married to one of David's soldiers, a Hittite named Uriah. While his troops were out on campaign, David uncharacteristically stayed behind. While he was out surveying his kingdom from his rooftop, he saw Bathsheba bathing on her own roof. He was immediately enraptured by her beauty and sent for her. Yet this was no consensual dalliance. The power dynamic between king and subject left Bathsheba with no real choice or agency in the matter. The king could not and would not be denied without consequences. For generations, many interpreters of this story have called Bathsheba an adulteress and seductress, when in fact she did not initiate the encounter and likely had no choice in the matter. This is not a story of a mutually consensual affair, but that of sexual assault and abuse of power.

After some time, Bathsheba sent word to the king: She was pregnant. David immediately knew what to do. He sent for Uriah and granted him furlough, expecting Uriah to lie with his wife and come to believe the baby was his. Problem solved. Uriah, however, refused to go home while his comrades were still on the battlefield, choosing instead to sleep in the king's doorway with the servants. David's Plan A was thwarted, so it was time for Plan B. He had his general Joab set Uriah up on the battlefield by sending him to the front lines, which led to his death. David then brought Bathsheba into his house and married her.

Although the child Bathsheba carried died soon after birth, she and David eventually had more children, including a son, Solomon. Solomon later succeeded his father on the throne, but not by right. He was not the eldest of David's sons, nor the next in line for the kingship. It was Bathsheba, together with the court prophet Nathan, who acted behind the scenes to convince David that Solomon should be his successor rather than his other sons. This is why Solomon, too, is featured in Matthew's genealogy as one of Jesus's ancestors.

WHAT IS MATTHEW DOING HERE?

This leads us to an important question: Why would Matthew buck convention and include the names of these women in his genealogy? There are several reasons we might suggest. First, each of these named women existed in a vulnerable state. Each one of them had experienced a series of unfortunate, unasked-for events that could have spelled the end of their story. All of them were without the protection of a male, which meant a lack of rights to inheritance, the real possibility of exploitation, and loss of social status and legal standing.

These four women are also tied together situationally. They had no real options in front of them, culturally, and if they had not taken initiative, they would have been totally dependent on the decisions the men in their orbit did or didn't make. Yet, each of them refuses to accept that scenario and instead takes a kind of bold action. All four of these women orchestrated a response to their circumstances that radically transformed not only their future, but the future of the people of Israel. Their courageous refusal to accept as final the hand they had been dealt or their society's shame was the catalyst that introduced some of Israel's greatest heroes. David, Solomon, and Josiah are key figures who significantly shaped the stories of Israel and Judah and would not have existed without these four brave women.

Notice also that all four of the named women give birth to these sons within the context of situations that operated outside of the sexual norms and expectations of their culture. Tamar used deception to trick Judah into fulfilling his family obligation. Rahab had become a prostitute, possibly because she had no other viable options to provide a life for herself. Ruth took an active role in pursuing Boaz, and Bathsheba responded to an abuse of David's kingly power by working behind the scenes to maneuver her son Solomon onto the throne.

These women also represent outsiders who become not only welcomed into Israel but key participants in shaping the future of the people. Each of them, even though not all Israelite in origin, ends up identifying with Israel and, crucially, with Israel's God.

The first three, Tamar, Rahab, and Ruth, are all Gentiles, and they are each from a particular people that were experiencing hostilities with Israel—Canaanite, Jerichite, and Moabite, respectively. While Bathsheba was not a Gentile herself, her husband Uriah was a Hittite who served in David's army. Though not originally from Israel, the very name Uriah implies that he had, at some point, embraced the worship of Israel's God. A detail that we don't notice in English, but that would be obvious in Hebrew, is that Uriah contains what scholars call a "theophoric element." That's a fancy way of saying the name of Israel's God, Yahweh, was included in the name Uriah, which implies reverence and worship of that God. Bathsheba became, for Matthew, an early symbol of the diverse community that would become the church.

The inclusion of these women points to how Jesus will redefine and reimagine the meaning of family later in Matthew. In chapter 12, we find Jesus speaking to a crowd, and we learn that his mother and siblings had come to see him. Pay close attention to how Jesus transforms the meaning of family in his response:

> *Someone told him, "Look, your mother and your brothers are standing outside, wanting to speak to you." But to the one who had told him this, Jesus replied, "Who is my mother, and who are my brothers?" And pointing to his disciples, he said, "Here are my mother and my brothers! For whoever does the will of my Father in heaven is my brother and sister and mother."*
>
> *(Matthew 12:47-50)*

Family, for Jesus, was no longer strictly about his family tree or biology. He was developing a new understanding of family belonging tied to faith and participation in the kingdom of God movement.[6] The story of each of these named women reflects that same kind of redefinition, a belonging created as they aligned themselves with the God of Israel, regardless of their origins.

Matthew's genealogy culminates with a fifth and final named woman: Mary, the mother of Jesus. Perhaps Matthew's greatest goal in this genealogy that culminates with Mary is to insist that, like in Israel's past, a birth—and the child being born—can be holy, even when the context is less than ideal or pristine. The circumstances of his birth do not determine or disqualify him from doing the work of God in the world. In fact, Matthew is making the case that God has long been known to work in and through people and unexpected situations, even unexpected pregnancies.

AN INVITATION TO WHAT IS POSSIBLE

It feels somewhat obvious that, by the time Matthew wrote his story, Jesus's paternity had come into question. Jesus has the name of a father attached to him beginning in Matthew, but not earlier in Paul or Mark. What rumors were swirling? What was being whispered about Jesus's origins? We find perhaps a hint of what was being said in the work of the second-century philosopher Celsus, whose words are preserved only as quotations in the writings of Origen, a theologian of the second and third centuries. To counter his claims, Origen tells us that Celsus believed Jesus's mother had become pregnant by a soldier named Panthera, and as a result, she was rejected by her carpenter husband.[7] While Celsus's work was written almost one hundred years after Matthew, it at least helps us understand that Matthew may have been addressing similar questions about Jesus's paternity when he wrote in the 80s.

What is fascinating is that Matthew does not ignore the possible whispers and murmurs. Instead, he leans into them by elevating four other women of connected experience who, as we've seen, engaged in heroic actions that saved the future of the people of Israel. Matthew then adds Mary's name to the list because he believes that her son, Jesus, regardless of the potential rumors, had done the same. Jesus was God's saving, liberating Son born into the world, even if the circumstances seemed somewhat nebulous.

This is why I love Matthew's genealogy and never skip reading it during Advent. It makes the bold claim that God always works in unconventional ways, through sometimes surprising people and situations, to bring about God's liberative and transformative dream for the world. Advent, my friends, can still change the world, because we are still in need of this kind of hope and conviction. When we feel knocked down or knocked out, unworthy and impossible, Matthew would argue it is in just that moment that we are actually ready to join God in the beautiful, hopeful thing that God longs to do in the world. That is the continuing gift that Matthew's genealogy offers us. These "begats" and "begots" are not filler or preamble for the real story. They are an invitation to see our own challenging, flawed, imperfect, and even unjust experiences as being somehow transformed into something hopeful, full of potential and possibility, that just might change us and the world.

CHAPTER 3

LIKE A KID AT CHRISTMAS

CHAPTER 3

Like a Kid at Christmas

Kids get ridiculously excited about Christmas. That is not a groundbreaking observation, is it? We even use the phrase "like a kid at Christmas" to describe a level of excitement that transcends the ordinary. While this is broadly true, my youngest child reaches levels of Christmas hype that may never have been seen before. For many kids (and adults, like yours truly), the excitement for Christmas hits sometime after Halloween. After they've eaten their trick-or-treat candy, they know that all that stands between them and holiday fun is Thanksgiving, so they begin making lists and dreaming about what they might unwrap on Christmas morning. Not my kiddo. He starts in January. Before we even take down the decorations, he's already planning, scheming, and dreaming about next Christmas. He keeps a growing, detailed list throughout the year and, by late spring, is asking the regular question, "How many days until Christmas?" His enthusiasm is contagious, and eventually it spreads to all the other kids in the house, who also begin tracking the days that stand between them and their Christmas dreams coming true.

However, not everyone shares his joy at the coming of Christmas. In Matthew's Gospel, the news of Mary's pregnancy is not met with the same enthusiasm, at least at first. After Matthew completes Jesus's genealogy, we are introduced to a man named Joseph, who will be a central figure in this earliest Christmas story. This is an important moment because it is the first time in our written sources that Jesus's father has been mentioned or given a name. If you recall, Mark refers to Jesus as "the son of Mary," his mother, but makes no mention of a father.

What, then, do we know about Joseph? Not very much. He appears here in Matthew, again in Luke chapters 1 and 2, albeit more as a background character, and in a couple of references to Jesus as Joseph's son in John. He is present in the Christmas stories, but after Jesus was age twelve, he disappears from the scene. While that sudden departure has led to quite a bit of fan fiction that seeks to explain his absence—that he was older and had died, for example—it might also be that he has served his purpose in these birth stories, and the authors felt no need to explain what happened to him. The point is not Joseph, after all, but how Joseph's actions impact Jesus's birth. To understand that, we need to think about that name, Joseph.

JOSEPH ENTERS THE STORY

When Matthew brings Joseph into the picture, he does so by telling us who his father was:

> *. . . Jacob the father of Joseph the husband of Mary, who bore Jesus, who is called the Messiah.*
>
> *(Matthew 1:16)*

As we noticed earlier, Luke gives a different name for Joseph's father. Instead of Jacob, Luke tells us that Joseph's father was named Heli. While some interpreters twist themselves into a pretzel trying to find a way to make these two different names for Jesus's grandfather align, there are likely theological reasons for the difference.

The two genealogies are quite different from one another and not just in this one detail. For example, Matthew begins with the genealogy, while in Luke, it follows Jesus's baptism. The two family trees also move in different orders: Matthew from past to present, and Luke from present to past. Further, Matthew traces Jesus's lineage only to Abraham, which makes sense because he is telling his story of Jesus likely with a Jewish audience in mind. Luke, thinking more broadly about Jesus's appeal to Gentiles, tracks Jesus's line all the way back to Adam, the first human in the biblical narrative. Finally, other names, not just Jacob and Heli, are contrasted with one another. Instead of trying to make these two distinct genealogies match up, it is far more interesting to let them stand on their own, which allows us to hear each author's unique message and interpretation of Jesus's life. Our focus in this chapter is on Matthew's Gospel, so let's take a look at his use of Jacob as the father of Joseph and ask what it might mean for the story he is inviting us to hear.

Does this pair of names, Jacob and Joseph, ring any bells for us? Are there any other stories in the Bible that bring these two names together? The answer is illuminating for how we understand the story because Matthew wants us to see Jesus within the larger tradition of his ancestors. Jesus is not starting a new religion, a fact about which Matthew is extremely clear.

In his Sermon on the Mount, Jesus explicitly tells his listeners that he is not attempting to abolish the Law and Prophets but, instead, to fill them up with meaning:

> *"Do not think that I have come to abolish the Law or the Prophets; I have come not to abolish but to fulfill."*
>
> *(Matthew 5:17)*

If we look back into Israel's past, we discover this same pairing of names, Jacob and Joseph, in the early stories of the Patriarchs. You might recall the big three we meet in Genesis: Abraham, Isaac, and Jacob (Jacob would eventually have his name changed to Israel by God after an intense wrestling match between the two in Genesis 32). Jacob had twelve sons, who went on to become the twelve tribes of ancient Israel. One of these sons, his clear favorite, was named . . . any guesses? You guessed it, Joseph, of the "Technicolor Dreamcoat" fame.

There are three key facts about Joseph that we should note. First, he had a father named Jacob. Second, he was known as the "dreamer," because God spoke to him through his dreams. Finally, his story culminates in saving his family from certain death (due to famine) by bringing them down to Egypt, where he was taken after his brothers sold him into enslavement. I do not think that Matthew is just picking any old name for his genealogy because, as we will see, in Matthew's birth story, Joseph has the same biography as his namesake: He has a father named Jacob, God communicates with him through dreams, and he will take the endangered Christ Child down into Egypt to protect him from harm. By including Jacob in his introduction to Joseph, Matthew connects to Israel's past and shows how Jesus is grounded in the stories and traditions of his ancestors.

After the genealogy, Matthew explicitly names the tension he alluded to by including Tamar, Rahab, Ruth, and Bathsheba in Jesus's ancestry. Joseph, he tells us, was engaged to be married to Mary when a shocking revelation occurs: Mary is pregnant, and Joseph is not the biological father. They had not yet consummated their relationship, so this presented Joseph with a serious decision to make. How would he respond to this unexpected and, to be honest, likely unwelcome news? He decided to act in a way that the Law prescribed as just and that he saw as compassionate. A betrothal was both a legally and culturally binding agreement, but he would not expose her to public disgrace. He chose to divorce her, quietly, instead. Before we condemn his decision, remember that we, the readers, have been privy all along to an important detail that Joseph has not: Mary was "found to be pregnant from the Holy Spirit" (Matthew 1:18). We aren't told how this information was discovered here; that is a scene Luke will include in his story, but Matthew does not. However, the Holy Spirit's involvement was announced, Joseph apparently hadn't received the memo.

As Joseph made plans to divorce Mary, he experienced a disruption in the form of a dream in which an angel disclosed to him that Mary was not unholy, but just the opposite. She would bear a son, through the power of the Holy Spirit, who would be a savior for the people. Joseph responded by following through with the marriage to Mary and embracing Jesus as his son. That decision no doubt brought with it a cost, particularly a social one. Were there whispers? Did the town gossips murmur? Assuming Joseph was an artisan of some sort, did he lose out on business in the fallout? How was Mary treated by the community? We can't know, but it seems likely there were social and relational implications. Yet, in the face of uncertainty and the range of potential consequences, Joseph stood by Mary and embraced the vocation to which God had invited him. He would, like his ancestor Joseph before him, act to keep his family alive and safe from harm in a time of danger and fear.

That is the story Matthew tells in a snapshot, but as you probably suspect, there is so much to explore and so much meaning to mine from this story. In his birth story, Matthew introduces themes he will flesh out in the remainder of his Gospel, which means it's not just introductory material, needless filler before he gets on to the important stuff. He's letting us know, right up-front, who Jesus is for him. But to understand how Matthew sees and interprets Jesus, we have to talk about Moses.

JESUS AS MOSES 2.0

In some ways, Matthew's goal of casting Jesus as a "new Moses" is obvious with even a cursory reading of the Gospel. The story of Herod's Massacre of the Innocents that sends the child Jesus into Egypt is clearly mirroring Pharaoh's attempt to prevent the infant Moses from becoming the liberator of the enslaved Hebrews. We will explore that further in the next chapter.

Additionally, the story and actions of the adult Jesus are built upon a Mosaic template. Notice these details in light of the story of Moses: Jesus came up out of Egypt and into the waters of baptism, reenacting the Exodus and crossing of the sea, both Moses-led events. Then, after coming through the waters, Jesus was led by the Spirit into the wilderness for forty days of fasting and testing that would determine exactly what kind of messiah he would be and the kind of kingdom he would announce. That is an echo of Israel's forty years of wandering in the wilderness. While in moments they gave in to those times of testing in the wilderness, Jesus would not.

The collection of teachings we know as the Sermon on the Mount also reflects this connection to the story of Moses. Matthew tells us that Jesus went up a mountain to preach to the growing crowd that was following him, which reminds us of Moses's experience on Mount Sinai. According to some scholars, this section of teaching, which spans three chapters in Matthew (5–7), represents the first of five distinct blocks of content in Matthew, an allusion to the five books of the Torah, traditionally attributed to Moses. Jesus is not offering a new Law so much as inviting his listeners into a deeper understanding of and a heart-centric engagement with the Law of Moses.

There are also not-so-obvious connections between the story of Moses, specifically his birth, and Jesus's birth story. In the Jewish tradition known as midrash, biblical stories are interpreted, expanded, and retold to explore deeper meanings, fill narrative gaps, and draw ethical, legal, or theological lessons. Midrash does not simply retell a story. It engages creatively with Scripture, often imagining dialogue, motivations, or even events that the biblical text itself leaves unstated. In the later midrash tradition about the birth of Moses, Hebrew males in Egypt responded to Pharaoh's decree that all baby boys should be thrown into the Nile River by divorcing their wives. They would take no chances that their children would become victims of Pharaoh's paranoia and violence. However, in a dream from

God, Moses's sister Miriam is told that her parents will give birth to a deliverer for Israel. She shared the dream with her parents, who decided to remarry and then produce a son who would become just that deliverer.[1]

Why would Matthew want to connect Jesus so closely to Moses? What about these two figures warranted such a bringing together of their stories? Let me suggest a few important connections. First, Moses and Jesus were both understood to be prophets who were proclaiming the possibility of a different reality. They were both in communication and being given a message from God to share with the people. In Exodus 3, we find the well-known story of Moses's encounter with God in the burning bush, which begins his vocation as God's mouthpiece, calling Pharaoh to liberate God's people from bondage. While Moses is a reluctant prophet, resisting the call and requiring his brother, Aaron, to serve as his mouthpiece, he eventually goes to Egypt to proclaim God's liberation to the world's most powerful ruler.

Likewise, Jesus is presented in Matthew as the one who would act to liberate Israel:

> *"She will bear a son, and you are to name him Jesus, for he will save his people from their sins."*
>
> *(Matthew 1:21)*

Here we see how Matthew understands not only Jesus being like Moses but also, in some ways, including and transcending him. Instead of liberation from enslavement alone, Matthew says that Jesus would be the one to "save his people from their sins." Assuming the information from the previous chapter about what salvation/savior meant, we should also note that in the biblical tradition, sin was not just the personal disobediences, failures, or transgressions of individuals. Sin might include those things, but it speaks more to the systemic and corporate ways we have gone off the rails. In the biblical imagination, sin was not just about personal guilt but more about the societal and relational ways we create and perpetuate systems of injustice, harm, and violence.

The prophetic calling of each led them into the role of deliverer. Moses went into the belly of the empire's beast and demanded the freedom of his people. The result was one of the central events in Scripture that gives the idea of salvation its meaning: the Exodus from Egypt. Matthew understands Jesus to be leading a new Exodus, leading his people out of the injustice and violence of empire and into a different way of being human together. The liberation led by Moses began with a meal and was followed by the Exodus from Egypt. In the story of Jesus, we find a similar pattern. Jesus gathers a crowd, teaches and heals them, and then enacts the path of nonviolent liberation by giving his own life away in nonviolent love.

Matthew's statement that Jesus would liberate his people "from their sins" is a really important detail. The first mention of sin in the entirety of the Bible is not in Genesis 3, as we often assume. The word *sin* actually never appears in that chapter, interestingly. Those first humans eating the fruit of the Tree of the Knowledge of Good and Evil is not called *sin*, but it does create the conditions for the first sin. If the result of eating the fruit of that tree lived up to the name the tree was given, then sin is ultimately about judging—making decisions about who is right and who is wrong.

Once we take the place of God in that decision-making process, we will also be tempted to decide who should live and who should die. The rotten fruit of the tree in Genesis 3 is fully realized a chapter later when the word *sin* does appear for the first time in Scripture: Cain deciding to murder his brother, Abel. To save his people from their sins, Jesus must save them—and us—from their propensity toward violence. The death of Jesus, as opposed to Jesus building an army and enacting a violent revolution, is key to Matthew's understanding of Jesus as savior from sin. Matthew, writing in the aftermath the disastrous Jewish revolt against Rome from 66 to 73 CE, wants to make clear that any real deliverance—the kind that reflects the will and heart of God—must be nonviolent.

Violent revolt had just left the community decimated, and Matthew is not just offering a "Jesus told us so" to his contemporaries. He's offering a continued warning: If we do not abandon the idea that we can kill our way to peace, to our desired world, we will continually meet this terrible fate. It happened again in the 130s when Rome was even more merciless during the Second Jewish Revolt. For Matthew, Jesus offers—in fact, embodies—a way toward actual liberation. By loving, feeding, healing, and creating inclusive communities, Jesus taught that the power of love was ultimately greater and more transformative than the love of power.

Finally, both Moses and Jesus had stories that were about something bigger than their own individual stories. Their lives were about creating communities that could transform the world. Moses was the impetus for the liberation of the Exodus, although Moses himself did not live to see the end of the story. He died in

Moab, seeing but never setting foot in the Promised Land. This scene at the end of Moses's life reminds me of the final speech given by Dr. Martin Luther King Jr., on the eve of his assassination. The speech, titled "I've Been to the Mountaintop," evokes the image of Moses as King, telling the crowd why he had found peace in the midst of the uncertainty before them:

> Like anybody, I would like to live a long life. Longevity has its place. But I'm not concerned about that now. I just want to do God's will. And He's allowed me to go up to the mountain. And I've looked over. And I've seen the Promised Land. I may not get there with you. But I want you to know tonight, that we, as a people, will get to the promised land![2]

Jesus, too, gave his life before the kingdom of God movement he proclaimed had ever been fully realized. In fact, we ourselves still live in the in between time of that fulfillment. The world is not yet the place Jesus envisioned and announced. Both Moses and Jesus would entrust their continued work to those closest to them. For Moses, that was Joshua, and for Jesus, it is us, his followers. At the end of Matthew's Gospel, on another mountain, the risen Jesus would appear to his followers and empower them to continue his work. That is the same work we are called to continue today.

For Matthew, Jesus is not reinventing the wheel but continuing and advancing an ancient story, the story of Moses and Israel seeking liberation. Our tendency to focus primarily on a disembodied, spiritual reading of these stories has caused us to miss a central message of the story of Jesus and of Scripture as a whole: the liberation of bodies, communities, and the possibility of human flourishing.

THE VIRGIN SHALL BECOME PREGNANT

In Joseph's dream, the angel says that the conception of Jesus as the liberator of Israel was the fulfillment of words written by the prophet Isaiah around seven hundred years before his birth. Before we look at the Scripture quotation itself, let me first offer a couple of comments on the idea of prophecy and how Matthew is reading and engaging the text.

Many Christians, myself included, were taught to understand the work of a prophet as predicting the future. In fact, up until I was in graduate school, this was probably the lens through which I understood the work of the Prophets in the Hebrew Bible. They existed to point to Jesus, and that was their only purpose. What a surprise for me to discover that their work was so much more than just predicting the birth of Jesus. Prophets, in the Hebrew tradition, weren't prognosticators so much as they were God's "check engine light" for the nation. When injustice became rampant, when the poor and vulnerable were being oppressed, and when the leaders of the people were wandering away from faithfulness to God, a prophet would emerge to speak on behalf of God and call the leaders and the nation as a whole to return to God, which meant enacting justice, compassion, and faithfulness. They were not looking into the distant future but the immediate present and near future, and they were offering a sobering assessment of how things were and what the consequences of not changing their ways could be. A faithful prophet was a fly in the ointment of the king and his administration.

After their experience of Jesus, his disciples would begin to read the Scriptures in a way no one had before. As they read their ancient texts, page after page, they began to find passages that caused them to remember Jesus. Could it be, they wondered, that Jesus was somehow embedded in these stories and songs all along, and it is now that their eyes began to see it at a deeper level. Their experience demanded that they reexamine and reimagine their tradition. So, when Matthew wrote his Gospel, he included many such references that he had discovered. For him, Jesus was the fulfillment—the filling up with meaning—of what came before.

As Matthew wrote, he recalled a story from the Book of Isaiah that felt more relevant to the moment he was telling Jesus's story. It was prophetic. The verse he quotes is Isaiah 7:14, and it reads as follows:

> *Therefore the Lord himself will give you a sign. Look, the young woman is with child and shall bear a son and shall name him Immanuel.*
>
> *(Isaiah 7:14)*

The actual wording of this verse from Isaiah often surprises Christians because it isn't exactly the same as the passage Matthew quotes. Notice the difference between how Isaiah reads and how Matthew quotes it:

> *"Look, the virgin shall become pregnant and give birth to a son,*
> *and they shall name him Emmanuel. . . ."*
>
> *(Matthew 1:23)*

Those two verses don't say the same thing, do they? The discrepancy in the spelling of Immanuel and Emmanuel is benign. The first reflects a transliteration from Hebrew, while the second does the same from Greek. It's a language issue, not a theological one. The key difference that people usually point out, and the one I bet you noticed right off the bat, is that in Isaiah we find that a young woman *is*, in the present tense, pregnant with a son, but in Matthew it is a virgin who *shall become*, in the future tense, pregnant. Those aren't the same things, are they? Not even close.

It never fails that around Christmas every year, content creators on social media start posting "gotcha" videos about Matthew's "misquoting" of Isaiah 7:14. Yet, bless his heart, Matthew is not being nefarious here. He is simply quoting from the translation of the Bible that is most readily available to him, just like most of us would.

Sometime between the third and second centuries BCE, a collective of Jewish scholars in Alexandria, Egypt, created a Greek translation of the Hebrew Bible, known to us as the Septuagint or LXX.[3] In this translation, they took the Hebrew text of Isaiah 7, which said that a young woman (*almah* in Hebrew) is pregnant, and translated it as a virgin (*parthenos* in Greek) shall become pregnant. Matthew isn't doing anything sketchy here; he's just quoting the text that he could read/understand that was available to him. There is no scandal or controversy. If we want to understand why this passage stood out to him, we should spend some time in Isaiah 7 to discover what about this text gave Matthew new insight into the Jesus story.

According to scholars, the first thirty-nine chapters of Isaiah reflect the context of the eighth century BCE, roughly seven hundred years before the birth of Jesus, which was a particularly tumultuous time in the region of Israel and Judah. The source of the chaos was a particularly powerful and brutal empire in expansionist mode: the Assyrians. The small kingdoms in the warpath of the burgeoning empire didn't have many good options in front of them, practically none that didn't end up with either their total destruction at worst or subjugation and vassalage at best.

This geopolitical reality is reflected in Isaiah 7 and 2 Kings 16, where the story is also told. In the episode captured in this chapter, the kingdoms of Israel and Aram (modern-day Syria) have allied against the Assyrian threat and are mounting a pressure campaign to bring the smaller kingdom of Judah into their alliance. Ahaz, the king of Judah, wants no part in such a scheme. He refuses to bring Judah into what he sees as an alliance doomed to failure and destruction. Pekah, king of Israel, and Rezin, king of Aram, did not take his rejection well, and in response, they brought their armies to the walls of Jerusalem and set up a siege against it. Their plan was to conquer Judah, depose Ahaz as king, and replace him with a leader more sympathetic to their cause. This news brought sheer terror to Ahaz and his administration:

> *When the house of David heard that Aram had allied itself with Ephraim, the heart of Ahaz and the heart of his people shook as the trees of the forest shake before the wind.*
>
> (*Isaiah 7:2*)

This is an ancient way of saying that Ahaz was shaking in his boots. How could the small kingdom of Judah resist the larger, more powerful kingdoms to their north? There was only one solution in his mind: reach out to the Assyrians for help and embrace what was likely inevitable anyway—becoming a vassal state to the powerful Assyrians.

Then the prophet Isaiah entered the picture. God told the prophet to take along his son, Shear-jashub, and to go meet Ahaz to give him a critical message: The fate Ahaz feared—the destruction of his dynasty—was not in the cards.[4] Isaiah told Ahaz that God would deliver him and the people of Judah from this precarious situation without depending on Assyrian help or intervention. All Ahaz needed to do was trust God.

Ahaz preferred the other method. He wanted Assyria to bail him out against his enemies. That's when Isaiah offers Ahaz a sign from God.

> *"Ask a sign of the LORD your God; let it be deep as Sheol or high as heaven." But Ahaz said, "I will not ask, and I will not put the Lord to the test."*
>
> *(Isaiah 7:11-12)*

While this might seem like a pious response from Ahaz, since testing God is off-limits (see Deuteronomy 6:16), it is, in reality, not. Ahaz has made up his mind already. He knows exactly what he's going to do, and Isaiah is simply forestalling the inevitable. Isaiah, however, had the grit and stubbornness of a true prophet, and he pressed the issue further:

> *Then Isaiah said, "Hear then, O house of David! Is it too little for you to weary mortals that you weary my God also? Therefore the Lord himself will give you a sign. Look, the young woman is with child and shall bear a son and shall name him Immanuel. He shall eat curds and honey by the time he knows how to refuse the evil and choose the good. For before the child knows*

> *how to refuse the evil and choose the good, the land before whose two kings you are in dread will be deserted."*
>
> (Isaiah 7:13-16)

What exactly is the sign being offered here? Is it the birth of a baby seven hundred years in the future? I don't know if that would help Ahaz very much in that tense moment. The sign of the young woman being pregnant is likely not just any young woman or any son that will be born. Many scholars believe the pregnant young woman is the king's wife, and the child is the king's heir. The pregnancy is a sign that God has not—will not—abandon Ahaz or the people of Judah. The dynasty is secure and will continue. This child will be a sign of God-with-them. All Ahaz has to do is trust God and avoid Assyria. Yet Ahaz did the exact opposite. His decision brought temporary relief; in the short term, Assyria saved Judah from its enemies. However, in the long run, it proved disastrous for Judah. Ahaz's fear and Assyrian involvement led to a loss of autonomy and political dependency on Assyria, evidenced by the heavy tribute demanded of Judah.

Why would this story speak to Matthew? Isn't Joseph in a similar situation? Facing the scandalous pregnancy of his betrothed, he must decide to either trust that God is up to something in all this, or he can divorce her quietly and move on with his life. Would Joseph follow in the footsteps of Ahaz, or would he heed the promise of the sign before him?

For Matthew, Jesus is also a sign of God's abiding presence with us. His birth a touchstone that reminds us that God has never given up on or abandoned us. There is something so striking and breathtaking about this idea of God being with us in the vulnerability of a child, isn't there? Human children enter the world with absolutely no survival instincts or skills. We come onto the scene unable to do anything for ourselves. We communicate through smiles and cries and rely on the people around us to keep us fed, changed, nurtured, and safe. That is an experience, in the Christmas story, that God knows well. In Jesus, we meet a God who does not thunder from the heavens but cries for his mother's embrace. God is found in vulnerability, need, dependence, and trust. God is with us, showing us how to be human in the fullest and most beautiful sense of the word.

Perhaps this is one of the questions Advent and Christmas ask of us each year. Will we trust that way of Jesus—the path of love, nonviolence, compassion, vulnerability, and peace—is the path that leads to a better world, or will we let fear and uncertainty cause us to descend into the doldrums of hate, violence, indifference, coldness, and chaos? Joseph compassionately and courageously said "yes" to his invitation. What will our decision be?

THE MEANINGS OF THE VIRGINAL CONCEPTION

When we talk about the birth of Jesus, we usually call it the Virgin Birth, but that is not how Scripture frames it. In Matthew and Luke, it is not a virgin birth, but a virginal conception. Many assume this event is the same as the Immaculate Conception, but that is a misunderstanding. In the Catholic tradition, the Immaculate Conception refers not to Jesus's conception but to Mary's. As Christian theology began to codify doctrines like original sin (more on that later), theologians came to realize that

Mary herself would need to avoid the stain of human conception as well. This led to the development of a doctrine teaching that God granted Mary a unique grace that kept her from sinning. That is not what is happening in Matthew's Christmas story.

According to Matthew and Luke, Mary conceived Jesus before she had ever known a man (in the biblical sense). While many Christians vigorously defend this as a literal event, I am often surprised that we never really ask the most important question. Whatever one believes about how literal or not literal these stories are, the central, but too often avoided question, is "What does it mean?" Why does it matter that Matthew claims Jesus was conceived by a virgin? Let me offer a few thoughts that have been helpful for me.

First, the point of this story is not about the mechanics of reproduction. Here's what I mean: My earliest memory of learning about the story, which was probably around the time I asked "What is a virgin, and what does it mean to be a 'round John' virgin," was that Jesus had to be born of a virgin to bypass the stain of original sin. Is that familiar? For Jesus to be the sinless savior of humanity, Jesus could not be born in the same way we are, this perspective says, because we are born sinners. There are problems with this understanding. First, original sin did not exist as an idea when Matthew wrote. Remember, Matthew wrote his Gospel in the 80s, while the doctrine of original sin was not systematized until the late fourth to early fifth centuries by Augustine. Simply put, if we could take a time machine back to when Matthew wrote, and we asked him whether the virginal conception of Jesus was to circumvent original sin, he would look at us as if we had ten heads. It just wouldn't compute for him.

Beyond that, we now understand aspects of biology and reproduction that most humans in history couldn't have imagined. For example, many ancient theories of reproduction emphasized the formative role of the male. Thus, to eliminate the male component allowed Mary to carry the Christ Child without the stain of original sin. We now know that both male and female contributions are essential for reproduction. For Mary to carry Jesus would imply that her DNA was passed on to him. Original sin was not in the frame for Matthew when he wrote this story.

What might be the meanings, plural, of this story, then? Let me offer two that I find interesting. First, the birth of Jesus both includes and transforms the miraculous birth tradition of the Hebrew Bible. Beginning with the birth of Isaac to Abraham and Sarah, we find several unlikely births in the pages of Scripture. When Isaac was born, Abraham and Sarah had been unable to conceive and had reached the ripe ages of one hundred and ninety, respectively. That would set off a chain of unlikely and unexpected births: Jacob and Esau, Joseph, Samson, Samuel, and, according to Luke, John the Baptist. Each of these birth traditions followed a pattern: the inability of a couple to conceive, followed by a divine promise or angelic announcement of an impending birth. Also, each child was given a special destiny. The story of Jesus's conception and birth is firmly within this tradition, with a caveat. Jesus's birth was announced by divine promise and angelic announcement in both Matthew and Luke. Also, in both Nativity stories, Jesus's birth is given national importance, affecting all the people. As we saw in Matthew, Jesus will "save his people from their sins" (Matthew 1:21), and in Luke, he is given an even greater, if possible, pedigree:

> *"He will be great and will be called the Son of the Most High, and the Lord God will give to him the throne of his ancestor David. He will reign over the house of Jacob forever, and of his kingdom there will be no end."*
>
> *(Luke 1:32-33)*

There is one key difference in the birth stories that came before Jesus's, however. Jesus was not born to a couple dealing with the impacts of infertility. Jesus was born to a mother who was a virgin, as if to declare that something new was beginning. We must pause here and say that too many readings of the story of Jesus descend into antisemitism and supersessionism, the idea that the church has superseded Israel as "God's chosen people." All readings like this must be rejected. Matthew was, himself, Jewish, after all!

Could it be that at least one meaning of the virginal conception is that in Jesus God was announcing a new beginning, but one that was in continuity with what came before? Remember, Jesus did not break with the past. He reclaimed it and at times offered a reimagined understanding of it, yes. Yet, Jesus was thoroughly Jewish, and he never abandoned that identity. For Matthew, the birth of Jesus is the beginning of something new and transformative. It was the birth of renewal and redemption that called his readers back to the core of their faith: faithfulness to God, as expressed and evidenced by faithfulness to one another.

By quoting this passage from Isaiah, Matthew calls our attention to the new-but-in-continuity thing God was doing in their midst—and in ours. The story of Jesus's birth was not out of left field for Matthew. It was where this had always been heading. A Savior born to bring peace on earth. An heir to rebuild David's fallen tent. A Messiah who would usher in God's dream for the world.

I really understand why many modern Christians wrestle with this story and find it difficult to digest. God knows, I have experienced that same tension with this story. However, there is something going on here that is far deeper than arguments about what literally did or didn't happen—an invitation to participate in the birthing process of a different world, a world that deep in our bones we long for, even if we can't fully articulate it. That is the vision Matthew points to in his virginal conception story.

MATTHEW'S INVITATION TO US

The theological question at the end of every discussion is a practical one: What does this mean for me, today? How does the story of Jesus's conception and birth in Matthew's Gospel still speak and challenge us today? The story we've explored in this chapter offers us several invitations or challenges, depending on how they strike you.

First, Matthew's story invites us to dream new dreams. Matthew's Nativity story contains five dreams, four of them given to Joseph. Each of these dreams plays a key role in bringing Jesus into the world. I do not believe those dreams are only meant for the past. Creating a better world will require people with the courage to dream new, perhaps seemingly impossible, dreams and then be committed to the action needed to make those dreams a reality.

Each year during Advent, I am reminded of the audacity of such dreaming. I have a handful of friends who are committed, passionate gardeners, and they take their work seriously. If my family ends up planting a couple of raised beds, we usually don't even think about what that might entail until spring has sprung and the weather is warm. Not my serious gardening friends. Every year during Advent, they start posting excitedly on social media about the arrival of their seed catalogs. When creation is experiencing decay and slumber, they are plotting and planning for the new life that spring will bring. It has become a symbol of resistance for me.

When death and doom have us most tightly in their grasp, we need people who are dreaming of spring and have the faith to plant seeds, even when the ground is cold and hard. We cannot wait to dream until the conditions are right. They never will be, really. Advent calls us to a kind of dreaming that seems preposterous to the outside observer. Imagine Joseph explaining to someone why he was going forward with his marriage to Mary, even when the circumstances were, to quote the kids today, sus. Yet, he had been given a dream, and that dream had challenged and changed him in such a way that he could not shrink back from the invitation to join God in transforming the world.

What dreams are you carrying right now that need to be planted in good soil, nurtured, and given room to grow? That is an Advent question, isn't it? The genius of this season is that we celebrate the coming of the light precisely when the world is at its darkest. It is the stubborn insistence of hope that when all seems lost, God is still with us, fanning the embers of hope and inviting us to say "yes" to the work before us.

Speaking of that work, I am reminded that both versions of the Christmas story invited the consent of Jesus's parents. Joseph could have walked away from the moment. Mary could have too. They were both invited, called into an impossible situation, and they both had off-ramps. But they said "yes" to bringing Jesus into the world. What will we do when invited to the same task?

Meister Eckhart was a German Dominican friar, theologian, and mystic who lived in the thirteenth and fourteenth centuries. In one of his sermons, he spoke about the necessity of Jesus being born into the world again and again, across time and place:

> What good is it to me if this eternal birth of the divine Son takes place unceasingly, but does not take place within myself? And what good is it to me if Mary is full of grace if I am not also full of grace? What good is it to me for the Creator to give birth to his Son if I do not also give birth to him in my time and my culture?[5]

A modern paraphrase of this often goes something like this: "We are all meant to be mothers of God, for God is always needing to be born." This is the abiding invitation and challenge of Advent and Christmas to us. We are invited—called even—to bring Christmas past into Christmas present by giving birth to the Christ Child in our own times and places. What does that mean, however, to give birth to Jesus again in our own time?

It means the courage to say "yes" to the invitation to join God in the work of bringing a new world into being. It also means saying "yes" to the dreaming of new dreams, to planning gardens when the ground is frozen solid. This "yes" is how we begin to bring Christmas past into Christmas present.

CHAPTER 4

WHO'S COMING TO CHRISTMAS?

CHAPTER 4

Who's Coming to Christmas?

THE BEST PART OF CHRISTMAS

One of the best parts of Christmas in my childhood was our whole family being together. Every year, my out-of-town aunts and uncles, with my cousins in tow, would all come back to the holler in which they grew up, and where the rest of us still lived, to celebrate Christmas together. That was such a special time, and Christmas classics like "I'll Be Home for Christmas" always evoke a lovely sense of nostalgia and transport me back to those days at my grandparents' house in Appalachia. If I only had a time machine, I'd love to experience that for one more day.

The first Christmas wasn't all that different. In the two versions of the story we have, both include guests who come to behold and honor the Christ Child. In Matthew, we meet a group of distant travelers called *magi*. These out-of-town guests arrive at the home of Jesus and his family, bringing gifts to celebrate the newborn king. Luke introduces a different cast of characters at his manger, a group of shepherds who arrive at Jesus's make-shift delivery room to take in the wonder of the Savior's birth. In this final chapter, we will explore both stories to discover what they might teach us about Jesus, Christmas, and ourselves.

CHRISTMAS IN CONFLICT

Christmas is, for many people, a season to focus on peace. It's the one season of the year where it feels like the world might not be too far gone, that our differences are not deep enough to divide us forever. If you want to maintain that vibe, I have one piece of advice: Don't talk about what constitutes a Christmas movie. When this topic comes up, it's kind of like cilantro—no one is indifferent. People are passionate, fiercely so, about what is and isn't allowed to be categorized as a "Christmas movie." At the center of the debate is usually the movie *Die Hard*, a classic Bruce Willis action film from 1988. In the movie, NYPD officer John McClane is in Los Angeles visiting his estranged wife for Christmas when a group of terrorists interrupts her office Christmas party. I'll leave it at that so as not to spoil it for anyone late to the party.

I find there are two kinds of people in this debate. First, there are the people who think *Die Hard* is, in fact, a Christmas movie. Then, there are the people who are just flat wrong. *Die Hard* is a Christmas movie, and one of the first films I watch every year.

There are also other debates that get people to dig in their heels and passionately argue their position. At my house, one of these discussions centers on the kind of Christmas lights with which we decorate. I grew up using multicolored lights, and I absolutely love them, but everyone else in my house prefers the clear, basic white lights. Boring, I say. Every single year, there is a contentious conversation as we unpack the decorations, one in which I am the lone voice of joy.

We probably don't think of the first Christmas story as being one that includes conflict, but if we keep reading, we will discover that the birth of Jesus was not all calm and bright as we might imagine. After Matthew shares his brief account of Jesus's birth, which includes none of the core images we think of when we imagine the Nativity (the manger, lack of guest room, etc.), he turns to perhaps his best-known contribution to the Christmas pageants we enjoy each year. Outside of the quotation from Isaiah 7, Matthew's greatest Christmas addition is his story known as the visit or adoration of the magi. The action picks up immediately as we turn the page from chapter 1 to chapter 2:

> *In the time of King Herod, after Jesus was born in Bethlehem of Judea, magi from the east came to Jerusalem, asking, "Where is the child who has been born king of the Jews? For we observed his star in the east and have come to pay him homage."*
>
> *(Matthew 2:1–2)*

Who are these unexpected visitors who suddenly crash the party? From where do they come? What does it mean to be a magi? While these figures are shrouded in a bit of mystery, there are a few things we can say about them. First, nowhere in the text does Matthew call them kings. That detail is added to the story by accretion as certain texts from the Hebrew Bible are read into it, which might have been Matthew's goal all along. He is clearly alluding to images and texts from the Hebrew Bible in this portrait of the magi. There are three texts in particular that seem to lie behind this story and our assumption that these visitors were kings.

You might not be surprised to learn that the passages with the strongest connections to this story also come from the prophet Isaiah. Isaiah 49 is part of a section of the book (chapters 40–55) that reflects the context of the Babylonian Exile. In this chapter, the author is writing about the mission of God's chosen servant, who will not only redeem Israel but also be a beacon to the Nations.

> *"It is too light a thing that you should be my servant*
> *to raise up the tribes of Jacob*
> *and to restore the survivors of Israel;*
> *I will give you as a light to the nations,*
> *that my salvation may reach to the end of the earth."*
> *(Isaiah 49:6)*

The prophet continues, imagining the tables being turned and that the servant who has suffered under the powerful rulers of the world would someday be appreciated as the chosen representative of God in the world:

> *"Kings shall see and stand up;*
> *princes, and they shall prostrate themselves,*
> *because of the LORD, who is faithful,*
> *the Holy One of Israel, who has chosen you."*
> *(Isaiah 49:7)*

One final passage—this one, the most obviously being alluded to by Matthew—comes from Isaiah 60. This text is part of the final grouping of chapters in the book, Isaiah 56–66 and reflects the period of return from exile. The people are beginning to hope again and to imagine a different future. In the passage that follows, we will also discover where we get the idea that the magi journeyed to honor the Christ Child riding on camels, while Matthew never addresses their mode of transportation:

Arise, shine, for your light has come,
and the glory of the LORD has risen upon you.
For darkness shall cover the earth
and thick darkness the peoples,
but the LORD will arise upon you,
and his glory will appear over you.
Nations shall come to your light
and kings to the brightness of your dawn.

A multitude of camels shall cover you,
the young camels of Midian and Ephah;
all those from Sheba shall come.
They shall bring gold and frankincense
and shall proclaim the praise of the LORD.
(Isaiah 60:1-3, 6)

So, while not called kings, the passages that possibly lie beneath this story do use that language. If not kings, then what? Matthew most likely intends us to understand these visitors as astrologers and/or priests in the Zoroastrian tradition, likely from Persia. Their journey, then, would have originated in modern Iran, as they followed the star from the East. We will come back to this as we conclude our exploration of this episode.

A final piece of Bible trivia before we move on to explore the details of the story: We have traditionally assumed that there were three magi who visited Bethlehem, but nowhere does Matthew number them as three. It is likely that we make that assumption based on the treasures they brought to honor Jesus:

- Gold, a gift for a king
- Frankincense, used in worship
- Myrrh, used to perfume and to prepare bodies for burial

These gifts are not the kind you keep the receipt for or regift to a coworker. These are gifts that foreshadow who this child will become and where his story will take him. With the arrival of the magi, the drama and danger of the story are shifted into overdrive.

"STAR OF WONDER, STAR OF LIGHT"

These magi came to the region of Judea to search for the newborn king of the Jews, not because of a birth announcement from angelic visitors as we will see with Luke's shepherds. The journey of the magi is inspired by seeing "his star in the east" (Matthew 2:2). That "star" has become the focal point of so much Christian imagination over the centuries. This star is the melodic focus of the Christmas hymn "We Three Kings," as the travelers ask the heavenly body to guide them toward their desired destination:

O star of wonder, star of light,
star with royal beauty bright,
westward leading, still proceeding,
guide us to thy perfect light.[1]

Like many of you, I have vivid memories from my childhood, staring up at the early night sky on Christmas Eve, wondering which star it might be that led these seekers toward Bethlehem. There are some issues here, however. For example, we now understand that stars do not visibly guide travelers in the miraculous manner Matthew describes, as a kind of early GPS. Even then, astronomers and others tried to deduce what it might have been that they saw and followed. Was it a conjunction of planets that gave off a bright light? Some sort of comet or supernova? Maybe the rotation of the Earth gave the appearance that the celestial body was moving? I really understand the desire to find some rational explanation for a seemingly unexplainable phenomenon. However, I don't think science can help us on this one. While I run the risk of sounding like a broken record, if we want to understand the star that led the magi to the infant or toddler Jesus, we must remember Matthew's conviction—that to understand Jesus, you must look back into the Scriptures of his people. It was in the pages of the Scriptures, not the night sky, that Matthew's star was born.

There are two specific texts from which the star of Bethlehem comes to us. The first is found in Isaiah 60, which, as we've seen, portrays the Jewish exiles returning home and the nations around them ceasing their hostilities and embracing Israel's God.

> *Nations shall come to your light*
> *and kings to the brightness of your dawn.*
> *(Isaiah 60:3)*

The second possible passage that inspired Matthew is found in Numbers 24, and it is part of a very strange tale about a diviner named Balaam and his talking donkey.[2] Yes, you read that right. *Shrek* was not the first story to include such a phenomenon. In the story, Balaam had been commissioned by Balak, the king of Moab, one of Israel's most despised enemies, to place a curse upon Israel. In the end, however, Balaam does not curse Israel but pronounces several oracles of blessing upon Israel. The fourth of these prophecies took on messianic meaning and interpretation:

> *I see him but not now;*
> *I behold him but not near—*
> *a star shall come out of Jacob,*
> *and a scepter shall rise out of Israel;*
> *it shall crush the foreheads of Moab*
> *and the heads of all the Shethites.*
> *(Numbers 24:17)*

As you can see, this did not go at all the way the king of Moab had hoped. According to Balaam, one day a leader would emerge from Jacob (another name for Israel), and the image he used to symbolize that leader who would crush Israel's enemies was that of a star and a scepter. Not only did this imagery take on messianic meaning, but it also became a central theme during the Second Jewish Revolt against Rome, which began in 132 CE. The leader of the resistance was named Simon, but Akiva, a rabbi, called him Bar Kokhba, proclaiming him the Messiah. Bar Kokhba means "Son of the Star," a reference to this prophecy in Numbers 24.

For Matthew, the star of Bethlehem is far more significant than just an early form of GPS. It was a symbol. One way we can put it is that the star represents Jesus himself, the Messiah who would draw the nations to the God of Israel, just as the prophets imagined. However, according to some of the prophets, this was supposed to happen in tandem with God destroying Israel's enemies, such as Moab. Jesus, however, will embrace another vision. Matthew spends the rest of his Gospel presenting Jesus as a messiah who loves his enemies and experiences compassion for them. He doesn't crush them; he feeds them. He doesn't wound them; he heals them. He doesn't seek to subjugate them but, instead, offers the possibility of real liberation. The experience of Jesus—especially his unexpected (by them) death—caused many of his followers to reimagine what it actually meant to be the Messiah. The star of Bethlehem is a hint, a foreshadowing clue very early in the story that invites us to see the kind of messianic figure Jesus will become.

HEROD: THE VILLAIN OF CHRISTMAS

Every year, I change my Facebook cover picture during Advent to an image of a Nativity scene my kids created in 2020. Our younger kids were all under five at the time, and their ability to stay within the lines of the paper crèche we had cut out for them to color was slightly lacking. I wish you could see it. It is gorgeous in that nonobjective-dad-glasses kind of way. Sadly, the picture is all that remains of that labor of love. Shortly after they finished and we set it out with the other decorations, the family dog we had at the time decided to make her contribution. Her name was Lucy, and she was totally unhinged. She devoured it all—baby Jesus, his parents, the animals, even the stable. She was quite literally the Grinch who ate Christmas. Year after year, when I select that picture as my Facebook banner, I remember my kids at that age, our wild dog Lucy, and inevitably, my mind drifts toward Herod, the real villain of the Christmas story in Matthew.

The arrival of the magi sets up the central conflict not just of the Christmas story in Matthew but of the Gospel as a whole. I just recently noticed an interesting detail: the star does not first lead them to Jesus. It leads them to Herod. Perhaps they made the same assumption we might, that kings are born in palaces. Kings enter the world in the lap of luxury and are groomed for royalty. Jesus would not be found in any of Herod's palaces (and there was plenty from which to choose), but in a humble dwelling surrounded not by servants and wealth, but the love and joy of his parents.

When the magi arrived, they were probably surprised to discover that there was no vacancy for the position of king of the Jews. That role was occupied by Herod and had been since the Roman senate appointed him as king in 40 BCE. Herod always felt his power was under threat. Part of the reason the announcement of a newly born king of the Jews—a messiah—would be so troubling to Herod is that, first, he was not ethnically Jewish. His family was from Idumea, a territory neighboring Judea, and had converted to Judaism in the late second century BCE. Second, Herod was not from the line of David, and the Jewish hope was inextricably bound up with the true king of the Jews restoring the Davidic line to the throne. Finally, Herod, who was appointed by Rome, was viewed with deep suspicion and even contempt. He was a pro-Roman leader because Rome was the source and legitimator of his power. As a result, Herod benefited from a relationship with Rome that was harming most of his people. That, of course, created far more enemies than friends.

When the magi arrived and asked for directions so they could honor the newborn king, Herod had no clue where the child was supposed to be born. However, he did know exactly what they meant—they were talking about the birth of the Messiah, the rightful king of Israel who was chosen not by Rome but by God.

As you might expect, Herod did not receive the news of a newborn king with open arms. This posed a direct threat to his power and position—a threat that must not go unchecked. Herod's plan was solid on the surface. He would play nicely, give the magi the information they wanted, and send them off to find the Christ Child . . . with a caveat. He wanted to know the exact location of the new king, so he could go and honor him, too.

> *Then Herod secretly called for the magi and learned from them the exact time when the star had appeared. Then he sent them to Bethlehem, saying, "Go and search diligently for the child, and when you have found him, bring me word so that I may also go and pay him homage."*
>
> (*Matthew* 2:7-8)

Herod's plan was foiled by another of the dreams Matthew records. This is the only dream in chapters 1 and 2 that didn't involve Joseph but was instead given to the magi to warn them about Herod's actual plan to kill the child they were seeking.

> *When they had heard the king, they set out, and there, ahead of them, went the star that they had seen in the east, until it stopped over the place*

> *where the child was. When they saw that the star had stopped, they were overwhelmed with joy. On entering the house, they saw the child with Mary his mother, and they knelt down and paid him homage. Then, opening their treasure chests, they offered him gifts of gold, frankincense, and myrrh. And having been warned in a dream not to return to Herod, they left for their own country by another road.*
>
> (*Matthew 2:9–12*)

The magi completed their journey and took the backroads home to avoid tipping off Herod, who did not take their failure to comply with his wishes well. As a result, like Pharaoh in Exodus, Herod ordered that all children aged two and under be killed. He might not know who this child was or exactly where he was, but he'd wipe out an entire generation to be on the safe side. This is another example of Matthew engaging with existing midrash about Moses's birth to tell his story of Jesus. According to a text known as Pseudo Jonathan, a later Targum (meaning it is a Jewish Aramaic translation and interpretation of the Hebrew Bible) that preserves some older interpretive expansions of the story, Pharaoh had a dream in which the entire land of Egypt was placed on one side of a scale, and a small lamb on the other side. To his shock, the small lamb outweighed the entire land. Pharaoh's dream interpreters knew the meaning instantly: "A son is to be born in the assembly of Israel, through whom all the land of Egypt is destined to be destroyed."[3]

Just as Moses was saved by being placed into a basket and floated down the Nile, so Jesus was saved when Joseph was warned in another dream about Herod's plan. The Holy Family fled to Egypt to escape Herod's murderous plot, only returning and relocating to Galilee after the death of the wicked king. This descent to Egypt and return to Israel also reenacted the story of the Exodus. As we've seen, Matthew wants us to understand Jesus as embodying and recasting the story of Israel in a new Exodus for a new moment.

The question many people ask about this story, known as the Massacre of the Innocents, is "Did it really, historically, happen?" The truth is, we have no source outside of Matthew that recounts this awful story. Yet, these actions are very much on brand for King Herod. History tells us that Herod was both brilliant and mad. He was a creative builder, a shrewd politician, and also totally paranoid that others were trying to take his power and position away from him. That paranoia led him to kill his wife, his own sons, and countless others. While we have no evidence of this particular horror occurring, there is no historical doubt that it is very believable that Herod would undertake such an action. Matthew might be taking creative liberty, but it's grounded very much in the character and action of the historical Herod. In this way, Herod stands as an example of every fragile, power-hungry leader who has ever stolen, murdered, and harmed his own people for his own ill-gotten gain.

Let's leave Matthew's Christmas story with this closing image: a powerful, wealthy paranoid king on the one hand, and the innocence, vulnerability, and promise of the baby Jesus on the other. The Christmas story invites us to think about and wrestle with important questions: What does true power look like? Where do we find God in this story? In whose actions? How should this story inform how we understand and think about things like power and position in our own time and place? Will we become or be satisfied with self-centered and self-aggrandizing leaders who put our own interests above the common good, or will we choose a different kind of leader and a different kind of leadership? It seems obvious the choice Matthew hopes his readers, then and now, will make.

KEEPING WATCH BY NIGHT

When my parents brought me home from the hospital after I was born, my grandpa, whom I always called "Pop," met them in the driveway, took me from their arms, and took me in the house to meet the rest of the family. There is a picture on my phone, one I am so grateful to have, of him cradling me in his arms and looking down at me with a beaming smile. Needless to say, he and I were attached at the hip until his passing when I was almost twelve years old. There's just something about the joy of a baby, isn't there?

Just last week, at the time of this writing, some dear friends with whom I'm fortunate to learn and grow in our church community came up to me with wide grins stretching ear to ear. They had news, they said: They were expecting their first child. I don't know if I've ever seen a smile that joyful, besides my own, holding my own babies for the first time.

Sharing the news of a birth—recent or upcoming—is the height of joy. It's so important that the news is usually first shared with the inner circle of a person's or a couple's lives: parents, grandparents, siblings, dear friends. We have explored Matthew's first guests at Jesus's birth, the magi, but Luke does not seem to share the same affinity for them. In fact, twice, Luke mentions people he classifies as magi, and he does not present them favorably. In Acts 8, we meet a magician from Samaria named Simon, who, according to Luke, tries to buy the power of the Holy Spirit from Peter and John. They do not respond favorably, as you can imagine. The second mention is of Elymas, a Jewish false prophet who opposed Paul and Barnabas in Acts 13 and tried to subvert their work. Elymas's brief story ends with his being struck blind, an apt metaphor that Luke uses to interpret his actions. Magi will not visit the manger in Luke. Instead, in Luke's story, the announcement of Jesus's birth was first shared with a group of shepherds who stumbled into the joy of Christmas unexpectedly.

> *Now in that same region there were shepherds living in the fields, keeping watch over their flock by night.*
>
> *(Luke 2:8)*

Many interpreters assume that being a shepherd in the ancient world came with a sense of societal rejection and marginalization. In many ways, it was just the opposite during Jesus's life. Shepherds played a vital role in the economy of ancient Judea. They would, as the text in Luke suggests, spend time in open fields and wilderness grazing their flocks, which also meant protecting them from predators—lions, bears, wolves, and thieves. It was a dangerous job, but also an essential one. Their flocks were counted on to provide wool, food (like milk, cheese, and meat), and perhaps lambs for temple sacrifices in Jerusalem.

Not only did shepherds play a practical role in the life of the community, but their role evoked a continuity with Israel's past that can often be overlooked. If you recall, David, Israel's once and future king, was himself a shepherd prior to his ascension to power. That story is told in 1 Samuel 16 and echoed in Luke's inclusion of shepherds.

Let me briefly share the story with you. God had rejected Saul as king and had sent the prophet Samuel to Bethlehem to anoint one of Jesse's sons as the new king. This would need to be a covert operation, because Saul still occupied the throne and wasn't interested in abdicating any time soon. After Jesse's sons passed before Samuel, each one more impressive than the last, the prophet is surprised that God hasn't chosen any of these ideal specimens as the next king. Samuel was somewhat dumbfounded by the situation, but God called him to look beyond the external qualities and into the depths of the person.

> *Samuel said to Jesse, "Are all your sons here?" And he said, "There remains yet the youngest, but he is keeping the sheep." And Samuel said to Jesse, "Send and bring him, for we will not sit down until he comes here." He sent and brought him in. Now he was ruddy and had beautiful eyes and was handsome. The LORD said, "Rise and anoint him, for this is the one." Then Samuel took the horn of oil and anointed him in the presence of his brothers, and the spirit of the LORD came mightily upon David from that day forward.*
>
> *(1 Samuel 16:11-13)*

David, the shepherd boy, went on to become David, king of Israel. He lived larger than life in Israel's memory, an echo of who they used to be and a longing for who they could once again become. The prophet Amos imagined a descendant of David who would come along and restore and rebuild all that had been lost (see Amos 9).

That Davidic memory is also captured in the angels' announcement of Jesus's birth to the shepherds. Luke sets the angelic visit out in the fields and at night, and both details are interesting. First, shepherds living in the fields means that the weather is conducive to such an activity. That means that in Luke's imagination, this heavenly chorus is not happening in the wintertime, but in warmer weather. Second, the idea of night is symbolic. Just as the magi followed a star—a light—that would guide them to the Christ Child, the night sky in Luke 2 explodes with light and joy. The birth of Jesus was, for Luke, a pushback against the darkness in which his people were living under Roman occupation. The language is poetic:

> *Then an angel of the Lord stood before them, and the glory of the Lord shone around them, and they were terrified. But the angel said to them, "Do not be afraid, for see, I am bringing you good news of great joy for all the people: to you is born this day in the city of David a Savior, who is the Messiah, the Lord."*
>
> (Luke 2:9-11)

We've already explored the political meanings of "good news" and "savior," but notice the Davidic connection. Jesus was born in David's city, a significant pedigree to which the Herods of the world could not lay claim. The prophet Micah had envisioned a moment like this, a ruler arriving in Bethlehem to pick up David's mantle:

> *But you, O Bethlehem of Ephrathah,*
> *who are one of the little clans of Judah,*
> *from you shall come forth for me*
> *one who is to rule in Israel,*

> *whose origin is from of old,*
> *from ancient days.*
> (Micah 5:2)

How would these shepherds know when they had found the right child? Can you imagine them going door to door in Bethlehem in the middle of the night? They would not have to guess, however, because the angels offered them a sign:

> *"This will be a sign for you: you will find a child wrapped in bands of cloth and lying in a manger." And suddenly there was with the angel a multitude of the heavenly host, praising God and saying,*
>
> *"Glory to God in the highest heaven,*
> *and on earth peace among those whom he favors!"*
> (Luke 2:12-14)

In Matthew's quotation of Isaiah, a sign was offered: The young woman/virgin was pregnant/would conceive. Here in Luke, the sign is different; it is a child swaddled and lying in a manger. Both signs were indicators for those who saw them that this birth, this child, was sent from God.

The spectacle and angel song convinced the shepherds, and they went to Bethlehem to see for themselves this child about whom angels sing. Have you ever wondered who was watching the sheep? These shepherds apparently leave their flock to go and see the Christ Child. This is a moment that cannot be missed. Luke concludes this episode with a beautiful, intimate moment. The shepherds visit the Holy Family and share all that they had been told by the angels, then go back to the fields, but they don't return unchanged.

So they went with haste and found Mary and Joseph and the child lying in the manger. When they saw this, they made known what had been told them about this child, and all who heard it were amazed at what the shepherds told them, and Mary treasured all these words and pondered them in her heart. The shepherds returned, glorifying and praising God for all they had heard and seen, just as it had been told them.

(*Luke 2:16-20*)

As a parent, I can tell you the best gift I could ever receive is for someone to be kind and generous with my children. When someone takes time to notice how wonderful and special they are, it is a gift that cannot be quantified with a price tag. I really resonate with Mary in this moment, wanting to remember, to take it all in, to not rush past a beautiful moment like this. Daily, it seems I have those moments with my own kids. As they grow and stop saying certain words in certain ways, as they become more independent, as I watch them do things and then be so proud of their accomplishments, all I can do is follow Mary's example and treasure those moments.

We focus so much on the questions of divinity in the Christmas stories that we too often miss just how beautiful the humanity of these stories is. We call them the Holy Family, and yet they are also proud parents with a beloved child. Mary and Joseph are all of us, in some ways. They embody the human experience, with all the joy and pain of it. They are seeking to bring something of the divine into the world, and that's also what we are trying, however feebly, to do too.

What a powerful image with which to close our exploration of the Christmas stories, Mary and Joseph, gathered around the manger. The shepherds looked on with wonder and adoration.

The Christ Child, in all the vulnerability a baby brings, embodies the hopes and fears of all the years. It's incredible that, in two thousand years, we have yet to scratch the surface of all the meaning that Christmas offers to us.

FROM STORY TO MEANING

When taken together, these stories of the guests at the first Christmas offer us some important lessons that will be fleshed out and incarnated throughout Jesus's life. While not exhaustive, let me close by offering a handful of takeaways from the stories of the magi and the shepherds.

First, both of these stories reflect the kind of radical, inclusive welcome for which Jesus became known. In his public life, the Gospels portray Jesus as a deeply compassionate person who was willing to move beyond boundaries and barriers to embrace "the other." Those same notes are sounded in both birth stories.

The magi arrive, visitors from far away. They are not of the same religion, and we might even imagine a language barrier that prevents meaningful conversation. Yet, the experience transcended all the possible barriers and challenges. Mary and Joseph seem to have welcomed these travelers with hospitality, and they, in turn, reciprocated with generous gifts that held deep meaning.

Likewise, the shepherds were also welcomed to the manger after Jesus's birth. Can you imagine Mary, after the exhaustion and trauma of birth, hearing a knock at the door? Yet she and Joseph welcome the shepherds and hear their story, and it becomes a foundational moment that they would return to again and again, I'm sure.

The kind of radical welcome we find in the Christmas stories, beyond all the ways we carve up the world and separate ourselves from one another, can still change the world. At our core, beyond our labels, we are all human. We have similar hopes, dreams, fears, and anxieties. The latter can cause us to shrink our welcome and reject those who are different from us, but the invitation—and challenge—of the Christmas stories is to expand our welcome and to include all of God's children. When we truly understand what Jesus meant when he connected the love of neighbor, self, and enemy with our love for God, we glimpse his transformative vision for the world. According to both Matthew and Luke, Jesus's radical approach to hospitality began on the first Christmas.

Another application of the story of the magi that I have found particularly meaningful is focused on interfaith relationships. Remember, these magi who came in search of the newborn king were not from Judea, nor were they members of the Jewish faith. These magi came from another place, perhaps Babylon or Persia (both of which have a connection to the Jewish experience of the Exile), and they were practitioners of another religion. While we do not have a transcript of the conversation between these travelers and Mary and Joseph, what we see in the text offers us a template for a generous and generative interfaith relationship. The magi arrive and honor Jesus. They gift him with the treasures they thoughtfully brought with them. After paying homage to the child Jesus, these travelers turn around and make the journey home, back to their land and their traditions. There is no hostility expressed toward either religious tradition, no arguing about who is right and who is wrong. It is a lovely and profound moment of encountering someone from a different tradition, receiving the gifts they have to offer, and then leaving that encounter with all parties better for the experience.

This is an especially important skill to learn today. The world is getting smaller and smaller, isn't it? We all encounter people of different backgrounds and faith commitments in our everyday lives. We do not have to fear them, lash out at them, condemn them, or attempt to convert them. We can learn from one another, appreciate one another, and benefit from the exchange. Of course, there are people in all religious traditions who can show up in the world in hostility and harm. We just must remember that this is true of our own tradition as well. Far too many Christians behave in un-Christlike ways, and we must acknowledge that reality.

In her book *Holy Envy*, Barbara Brown Taylor references the "three rules of religious understanding" set forth by Krister Stendhal, a Swedish bishop and former dean of the Harvard Divinity School. In 1985, in Sweden, there was mounting tension and resistance among Christians over a new Mormon temple that was being built. At a press conference prior to the dedication of the building, Stendhal attempted to defuse the situation by offering three rules that would aid religious understanding. Those three rules, I think, still stand up and offer much to think about. They are

> When trying to understand another religion, you should ask the adherents of that religion and not its enemies.

Don't compare your best to their worst.

Leave room for holy envy.[4]

The story of the magi's visit beautifully shows how we can engage with people of other traditions in good faith and in ways that leave everyone better, enriched, and transformed by holy envy.

The Christmas story, particularly in Matthew, also offers a lesson for how we think about people in marginalized and dangerous situations that lead them to become refugees and asylum seekers. As I write these words, immigration is a hot-button issue, with some Christians vocally expressing disdain and hostility toward the stranger among us. Not only is Scripture replete with commands to care for the stranger and foreigner as we would ourselves, but the story of the flight into Egypt in Matthew also reminds us that Jesus and his family knew the precariousness of needing to escape a place that was unsafe and seeking to cause harm to them. After the magi leave for home by another route, shirking Herod's request to reveal the location of the newborn king, Joseph has a startling dream in which he is told to take Jesus down into Egypt to avoid the murderous plot Herod was hatching.

There are some interpreters who do not see this flight into Egypt as being the same as that of seeking refugee or asylum status, yet it meets the very definition of the terms as we use them today: The Holy Family fled their own country because of the danger of persecution and violence. This experience seems to have played a shaping role in Jesus's life in Matthew, especially seen in the parable of the sheep and goats in chapter 25. Jesus tells us that he would be present to them among the hungry and thirsty, the migrants and prisoners, the naked and the sick. From the journey to Egypt, to growing up experiencing the destructive impact of Roman economic policy in Galilee, Jesus knew the dangers of an inhospitable environment and called his followers, then and now, to meet him through our acts of compassion and our work to change the system that created the injustice in the first place.

One final takeaway from these stories is found in Luke's shepherds. They remind us that God has always worked in and through the ordinariness of life. While these shepherds are deeply symbolic of David, recall that David's own anointing as king was a lesson for the prophet Samuel that God is not impressed by impressive exteriors as much as receptive interiors. The shepherds were likely as surprised as anyone that they received the birth announcement that the Savior had been born. Yet that is just what happens in Luke. In an ordinary field, on an ordinary night, to some ordinary shepherds, the extraordinary happened.

I always appreciate the reminder that life is lived in Ordinary Time. When we think of the Christian calendar, the seasons to which we are often most drawn are the special times—Advent, Christmas, Epiphany, Lent, Easter, and Pentecost all receive special focus and attention. Yet, life is Ordinary Time, and the extraordinary happens far more often in the humdrum, monotony, and day-to-day of life. Christian spirituality is about learning to see and pay attention to the truth that the bush is always burning, God is always speaking, and every moment is brimming with potential for something new and beautiful to be born.

CHECKING ON THE BABY

When my first child was born, I was absolutely terrified. He was so small, and I just knew that I was going somehow to break this tiny bundle of God's best everything. From the moment we brought him home from the hospital, I developed a practice, a nightly ritual and routine of checking on him before I went to sleep. When he was very small, I'd go into his room, listen for him to breathe, and just watch him sleep for a moment. Sometimes I'd even place my hand on his chest to feel the rhythm of the rise and fall of his breath. To this day, I still check on all my kids every night before I go to sleep. Nothing invasive or dramatic. I'll just crack their door and peek in to see them safe, sound, and snuggled up. That is all going to be much harder when they're grown, but that is a bridge to cross another time.

When I think of the Christmas story, especially in Luke, I wonder if Mary and Joseph did the same. As they looked down at this unexpected and wonderful miracle they'd brought into the world, did Joseph ever place his hand on Jesus's chest to feel the rhythm of his breath? Did Mary bend down to kiss his forehead, both a gift of affection and also to make sure one last time that he didn't have a fever?

That is the power of the Christmas stories for me. We make them so "other worldly" sometimes, but they are really just so ordinary. They are stories about being human, stories about the love of parents for their child, and a reminder that God has always been found in the ordinary everydayness of life. Perhaps the greatest image of Christmas is not magi en route with treasures or the night sky exploding with angel song. Maybe the greatest image of Christmas is when, after all the guests have left, a mother and father check on their baby and realize what a gift they've been given. Christmas had changed their world and is still changing ours.

EPILOGUE

When I was a kid, I loved the Alvin and the Chipmunks Christmas album. My favorite song on the record was "Christmas Don't Be Late," because it tapped into a very real experience of children—it feels like it takes forever to finally get to Christmas. The anticipation and the excitement make the time between January and late December feel like a veritable eternity. We have even developed this as a metaphor for describing how long it takes someone to do something. Any time we attempt to leave the house, it takes longer than you might imagine for everyone to get their shoes on and grab whatever accoutrements they need for the journey, and I often will say, "You all are being slower than Christmas!" They know immediately, deep in their bones, what that means. Christmas, whatever you do, just don't be late.

As I look at the world around me, I feel that sentiment more and more deeply. In a world where hate, division, and bitterness seem so prevalent, Christmas feels like a time when all that is at least a bit more muted. Christmas, somehow, if ever so briefly, expands and softens the hearts of many people. There's no reason, however, that the meaning and gifts of Christmas can't carry on with us, even when the lights and tinsel come down and are stored in the attic until the next year. That is not up to the calendar; it's up to us.

In this book, I have attempted to do two things. First, I hoped to ground these familiar stories of Jesus's birth in their first-century context. That, as we have seen, is a world that is not all that unlike ours. The difference is that, along with many of my readers, I imagine, I have benefited from living in a global superpower, also known as an empire, in ways that Jesus could not have fathomed. By engaging the context, I hope you have come to see a different perspective on these stories. Second, I have offered several ways in which Christmas, an event of the past, can still change the world, all these years later. As we bring this study to a close, let me remind you of a few applications that are central, particularly for this season we call Advent.

During Advent, we focus on waiting, on preparing for the birth of Jesus and the celebration of Christmas. Yet waiting is not the same as passivity. The kind of waiting to which Advent calls is a waiting grounded in hope. It's a decision to stay present to both the beauty and pain of the world, a stubborn refusal to give in to the voices and forces that tell us that the way things are is just the way they must be. While refusing that cynicism, this hope is also not naive. It does not ignore, avoid, or pretend that all is well in the world. Instead, Advent hope believes—insists—that even in dark and difficult moments, the smallest acts of goodness and compassion that we enact are bringing a different kind of world into existence. This is the hope we cling to, live from, and are shaped by, which allows us to keep showing up and doing all we can, even as we also wait for that better world to be fully realized.

Advent is also a season focused on bringing peace on earth; but it's important to remember what that peace is like. It is not the peace through strength/violence of empire, a *faux* peace that is enforced to benefit the few at the expense of the many. It is the kind of wholeness that is present when all of God's children have enough and access to a fair share of God's good world. This kind of peace is made through a rejection of violence as a means to the desired end and a commitment to compassion, generosity, and pursuing flourishing for all people, everywhere.

One of the most absurd-seeming gifts of Advent is joy—the kind of joy that is not grounded in circumstance, but that functions as a kind of resistance against all the forces that attempt to pull us into cynicism and despair. This joy celebrates the birth of a child, even in the shadow of the empire. It's the joy that trusts that, even when we lack something, if we all come together in generosity and sharing, there is enough of God's good world for everyone. Paul framed this joy beautifully in 2 Corinthians. In chapter 6, he is outlining for the Corinthians the difficult experiences he's had as an apostle and herald of Jesus's good news, but it's not all gloom and doom. Notice how he ends this section:

> *We are treated as impostors and yet are true, as unknown and yet are well known, as dying and look—we are alive, as punished and yet not killed, as sorrowful yet always rejoicing, as poor yet making many rich, as having nothing and yet possessing everything.*
>
> *(2 Corinthians 6:8-10)*

For all the ways they've been mistreated, accused, and abused, Paul and his companions have found a rhythm of joy that transcends their circumstances and resists the creeping despair all around them. They might have nothing, but in profound ways, they possess everything that actually matters. My great hope is that we, in whatever situation we find ourselves in this season, find ourselves in communities that cultivate and tend this joy together.

Finally, Advent draws our attention to the greatest of all these things, the love that we experience in the story of Jesus's birth and the task before us of sharing it with one another. The challenge of the love we encounter in the Christmas story is that it is grounded in vulnerability. God among us, not as king or warrior, but as a helpless child depending on his parents to be fed, changed, and nurtured. Could love be anything else? Beyond posturing and image maintenance, the love that is born to us in this season meets us just as we are and loves us there. It also calls us to join in the work of sharing the goodness of this love with everyone we meet, somehow (God help us) even with our enemies. Remember, both the magi and the shepherds eventually left their moments of adoration and shared what they had experienced with others. May we embrace a similar vocation, not just during Advent, but always.

The power of the Christmas story is not just that it happened two thousand years ago. It's that it's still happening today. Jesus is still being born into the world through us—through our work to bring hope, peace, joy, and love to bear on the world God so loves. The reality is the world has (unfortunately) not changed all that much—powerful people still use their power to protect themselves at the expense of the powerless, after all—and the message and challenge of Christmas are still not welcomed by the Herods and Caesars of the world. May we, like Joseph and Mary, the magi and shepherds, welcome the good news of Jesus's birth. May we allow it to transform us and, with God's help, the world through us. That is, after all, how the meaning of Christmas past becomes Christmas present, when it is born through us. As we say "yes" to that invitation, we will find that Advent and Christmas still have the power to change the world.

NOTES

Introduction

1 There is a mention of Mary as Jesus's mother in Acts 1:14, but that is a companion volume to Luke's Gospel, so I don't consider it a separate mention.

2 Phillips Brooks, "O Little Town of Bethlehem," in *The United Methodist Hymnal* (The United Methodist Publishing House, 1989), 230.

Chapter 1

1 It's really just me. I'm people.

2 Priene Calendar Inscription (9 BCE), quoted in Marcus J. Borg and John Dominic Crossan, *The First Christmas: What the Gospels Really Teach about Jesus's Birth* (HarperOne, 2007), 160.

3 Borg and Crossan, *The First Christmas*, 159.

4 Augustus, *Res Gestae Divi Augusti: Text, Translation, and Commentary*, ed. and trans. Alison E. Cooley (Cambridge University Press, 2009), §13.

5 Cornelius Tacitus, *The Agricola and The Germania* (Oxford University Press, 1999), 30.5.

6 Borg and Crossan, *The First Christmas*, 159.

7 G. K. Chesterton, *What's Wrong with the World* (Dodd, Mead & Co., 1910), 48.

8 Mary Oliver, *Don't Hesitate, in Devotions: The Selected Poems of Mary Oliver* (Penguin Publishing Group, 2017), 68.

9 Oliver, *Don't Hesitate*, 68.

Chapter 2

1 "Hook," written by John Popper, performed by Blues Traveler, recorded 1994, on *Four*, A&M Records.

2 John Shelby Spong, "The New Testament: An Evolving Story," video, YouTube, June 2016, https://www.youtube.com/watch?v=igbKNLSxJ5k&t=1149s.

3 Gematria is a Jewish numerological system in which letters have numeric values, and words or names are understood to have numerical significance based on those values. In Hebrew, there are no separate numerals, meaning letters have numerical value.

4 Virgil, *Aeneid*, trans. David Ferry (University of Chicago Press, 2017), 6.790–94.

5 See Representative Lewis's post on Twitter from July 16, 2019, for more explanation of this idea of "good trouble" at https://x.com/repjohnlewis/status/1151155571757867011?lang=en.

6 This redefinition of what makes family, from biological origin to faith and participation in the kingdom of God movement, is referred to as *fictive kinship*.

7 Origen, Contra Celsum, 1.32.

Chapter 3

1 See chapter 5 in Borg and Crossan's *The First Christmas* for more on this midrashic story.

2 Martin Luther King Jr., "I've Been to the Mountaintop," speech delivered at Mason Temple, Memphis, TN, April 3, 1968.

3 Septuagint means "seventy," and LXX is the Roman numeral for seventy. Both refer to the number of scholars who worked on the translation (which was actually seventy-two in number).

4 *Shear-jashub* means "a remnant will return," so his inclusion in this story is to be both foreboding and hopeful. Judah might eventually be defeated, but it will not be completely destroyed.

5 Meister Eckhart, "Sermon 101," in *The Complete Mystical Works of Meister Eckhart*, trans. Maurice O'C. Walshe, rev. Bernard McGinn (Crossroad, 2009).

Chapter 4

1 John Henry Hopkins Jr., "We Three Kings," in *The United Methodist Hymnal* (The United Methodist Publishing House, 1989), 254.

2 The entirety of this story is outside of the goal of this chapter, but I encourage you to take a moment and read Numbers 22–24. It's fascinating!

3 Exodus 1:15 in Targum Pseudo-Jonathan: Exodus, trans. Michael Maher, in *The Aramaic Bible*, vol. 2 (Liturgical Press, 1994), 1.15.

4 Barbara Brown Taylor, *Holy Envy: Finding God in the Faith of Others* (HarperOne, 2019), 65.

www.ingramcontent.com/pod-product-compliance
Lightning Source LLC
LaVergne TN
LVHW032333100926
847860LV00040B/1832